The Pure Man's Devotional Guide

A Biblical Toolbox for Purity

Steve Etner

Learn more about this book
and its author by visiting our web site:
www.overboardministries.com

CONTENTS

Week Five: This is War!   83

FOREWORD

Forward. I love this word and this concept. I feel like a coach with a team who's about to engage a challenging contest. Or, perhaps more appropriately, an officer sending prepared but frightened troops into a tense battle.

Staying where you are is not an option. Retreat certainly is, but that only means that the battle must be fought on another day. Forward! Advance! Attack! Positive movement is the only real option.

I hope you feel this… the tension, the opportunity, the adrenaline, the desire to advance, to take ground, to engage the battle. There is no time for hesitation, second thoughts, or softness. The battle for purity is not just in front of you; it's all around. Gather your courage. Gird up your loins. Prepare for battle!

Why the language of warfare? Because purity is a battle. I'm a men's ministry guy and I hear stories regularly about the battle men face to live in purity. And—I hope this isn't a news flash—I have my own battles. I must guard my eyes, take captive every thought, and pray for courage and stamina in the battle.

The good news is this: there is help. And my friend and colleague, Steve Etner, is a veteran of this war. Yet he'll be the first to tell you that the battles continue. I'm thankful that he is not only willing to share his story with you but he's completely committed to helping you engage your battles and pursue victory.

In the following pages you'll meet Steve, hear parts of his story, and be encouraged by his pastor's heart. But, most importantly, you'll be challenged to grow comfortable and confident with the only weapon that will provide real help: God's Word. I'm amazed by Steve's knowledge of and dexterity with The Sword.

He'll help you understand the enemy's tactics and how to respond. He'll show you how to rightly handle the Word of God. He'll coach you in the battle and, as you move forward, you'll hear him shouting instructions and encouragement. Ultimately, *you* must pick up the weapon and become an expert; but you do so with confidence because you have a worthy King in Jesus and a master instructor in Steve.

The battle is on… Forward!

Mike Young
Founder & Executive Director
Noble Warriors

INTRODUCTION

Thank you from the bottom of my heart for picking up this book! Through the many ups and downs, twists and turns of life, I have seen God work in some amazing (and often unexpected) ways to unite people with the tools that can help them grow in their walk with Him. The fact that you have connected with this book is definitely one of them. There is a reason you picked this up. Whether it was the title, the picture on the cover, the text on the back, or some of the content within that you perused over, something within these pages resonated with your heart.

In view of the fact that you've begun reading this book, there are a couple of assumptions I am making about you. First, you (or someone you care about) desire victory in your life over the issue of sexual impurity. It's been a battle that you're tired of fighting. You have tried many times before and thought you were on the victory side, only to give in to the lure of lust, and falling back into old sinful habits.

My second assumption is that you are now beginning to understand that only God can help you know real, lasting victory over this sin, and you are ready to do whatever it takes. In fact, would you pause for a moment, right now, and take a look at Philippians 4:13 and compare it with Zechariah 4:6, Ephesians 3:16, and Isaiah 40:29-31? Awesome! If you want help in winning this battle, you've come to the right place.

A HORRIBLE NASTY ABSOLUTELY TERRIBLE DRAGON
For over 30 years of my life I was a slave to sexual impurity (Jn. 8:34). I constantly battled a three-headed dragon that I named LuPoMas (short for Lust, Pornography, and Masturbation). I fought, and I fought, and I fought. I gave in, and I gave in, and I gave in again. I read books on sexual purity, I went to pastors and counselors for help and guidance, and I prayed and prayed hard. Nothing changed.

Over 18 years ago, while on a business trip, I was in my motel room late one evening watching porn. Suddenly feelings of guilt and disgust washed over me. As I began bawling my eyes out, I lay prostrate, banging my head against the floor, pleading with God from the very depths of my being to please help me stop. I hated what I was doing and despised what I was becoming. I had lost control (not that I ever really had control to begin with). But no help came, no change happened in my life, and I continued to lust after porn and masturbate.

Let's pause for a moment to ask a very important question. In that motel room, did God forsake me? As I cried out to Him from the depths of my being, did He turn a deaf ear? Throughout any part of my life as a Christian, did God abandon me because of my sin? Did He say, "Steve, you're just not worth rescuing anymore"? No, no, and again, NO!

The God of Moses and Joshua is the same God today who "goes before you. He will be with you; he will not leave you or forsake you. Do not fear or be dismayed" (Deut. 31:8 ESV). He knows the battle you are enduring. He hasn't left you to white-knuckle your way through it alone. He is right here, right now, fighting by your side. I know that at times it doesn't seem like He is, but He who does not lie (Num. 23:19; Heb. 6:18) has given you His word and you need to trust Him.

Our amazing God has given you everything you need to be free from this beast (2 Pet. 1:3). Don't be afraid of charging in and taking back the ground the enemy has stolen from you. Yes, it will be hard. Yes, there will be strife—but there is also victory because "he who is in you is greater than he who is in the world" (1 Jn. 4:4 ESV)!

The God of today is the same God King David spoke about when he said, "The LORD will not forsake his people; he will not abandon his heritage" (Psa. 94:14 ESV). As a child of God, you are His heritage— you belong to Him because He purchased you at a costly price (1 Cor. 6:19-20; 7:23). He will not leave you behind because you keep giving in to the same temptation again and again. He loves you. He died for you. He wants you to trust in Him completely. He wants you to be free.

God "loves justice; he will not forsake his saints" (Psa. 37:28 ESV). He "will not forsake his people, for his great name's sake, because it has pleased the LORD to make you a people for himself" (1 Sam. 12:22 ESV). This is why we can be

> …sure that neither death nor life, nor angels nor rulers, nor things present nor things to come, nor powers, nor height nor depth, nor anything else in all creation *(including lust, pornography, and masturbation)*, will be able to separate us from the love of God in Christ Jesus our Lord. (Rom. 8:38-39 ESV, italicized addition mine)

No, God didn't abandon me or forsake me. He never has and He never will. He was right there beside me in that motel room, just as He has been every moment of my life. He heard my cry that night—as well as every cry I have ever made—and His heart wept right along with me.

God didn't leave me, but I left Him. I chose to stumble along the dark paths of sexual sin on my own. I am the one who decided to put Self on the throne and fill my mind with lustful images; then, through masturbation, I would give my offering of worship to a false god on an imitation altar. In my strong-willed, self-centered stubbornness I lived a life of idolatry and adultery.

Had you been a fly on the wall in that motel room—watching me cry out to God, hearing me sob like a broken man—you might have assumed I was repentant. Unfortunately, you would have assumed wrong. God doesn't look on the outward appearance. He wasn't impressed with my head banging and gut-wrenching sobs. The words coming out of my mouth didn't move Him to do something out of mercy on my behalf. That act, just like so many before it (and after it) was just that—an act. God doesn't look at what we do; rather He looks on our heart at what we are (1 Sam. 16:7).

Listen to these words from Hosea 7:14. God said, "They do not cry to me from the heart, but they wail upon their beds" (ESV). That was an apt description of me. I was wailing, but I wasn't crying to God from my heart.

Every time I called out to Him for deliverance, God saw a man who was tired of fighting, but not willing to yield. God saw a man who wanted the Miracle Worker to wave His "magic wand" and make the problem go away. God saw a man who still wanted to keep self on the throne, and who just wanted the Wizard of the Word to cast a spell on him that would remove the wrong desires and leave the right ones. But God typically doesn't work that way.

My "heart was not steadfast toward him" (Psa. 78:37 ESV). I was drawing near to God with my mouth and even honoring Him with my lips, but my heart was far from him. I was "fearing" Him because I knew that's what a good Christian man was supposed to do (Isa. 29:13).

THE SWORD THAT TOOK DOWN THE BEAST

So what made the difference? What brought about real change in my life? Let me draw your attention to what God says in Isaiah 42:16. "I will turn the darkness before them into light, the rough places into level ground. These are the things I do, and I do not forsake them" (ESV).

Consider carefully what God said He would do (and not do). God typically doesn't do the work *for* us; He turns on the light (Psa. 119:105) and shows us how to do the work (Psa. 18:34; 144:1). He equips us with the tools necessary to get it done (Heb. 13:21; 2 Cor. 9:8; Eph. 3:20-21) and He teaches us how to use them (2 Tim. 3:16-17).

It was *my* responsibility to walk the path. *I* had to travel the rough places—He wasn't going to carry me. He was, however, going to shine the light of His glory on that darkened path so I would know where and how to walk in a way that would always honor and glorify Him (Psa. 32:8; Prov. 3:5-6). He wasn't going to remove the obstacles that tempt me to lust. Rather, He would show me where the obstacles were and direct me in how to circumnavigate them (1 Cor. 10:13), giving me the strength needed—*when* needed—to hurdle them when necessary (Phil. 4:13).

A few years ago God brought a godly man into my life named Roger. Roger wasn't a pastor or a professional counselor, he was just a man sent from God into my life who had a love for the Father and a passion for Scripture. Week after week Roger would sit down with me and open the Bible. Week after week he would challenge me from

God's Truth. Between our meetings I had to read, study, and memorize God's Word.

That process was the catalyst for lasting change in my life. Through Scripture, God changed my thinking. As my thoughts began to focus more and more on my Savior, Redeemer, Father, and Eternal Friend, those same thoughts were less and less centered on self and what I thought I wanted and "needed" in my life. I began to seek out ways to honor God instead of gratifying myself (1 Thess. 4:1, 3-6).

Please understand, my friend, that to know real, lasting victory over lust and sexual impurity, you must be in God's Word daily. Not just reading it, but studying it, memorizing it, meditating on it, and then obeying it (Psa. 119:9). The things we think about will eventually become the things we do (Prov. 27:19). Only God's Word will help us focus our mind around things that truly matter (Heb. 4:12). Only Scripture—the Sword of the Spirit (Eph. 6:17)—will take down that horrific beast. That is why I wrote this devotional guide. That is why every page of this book is centered on God's Word.

THINK, THINK, THINK
Proverbs 23:7 says, "As a man thinketh in his heart, so is he" (KJV). When my mind was fueled by lust, when my thoughts were focused on what would make me "feel good," my actions were bent on finding ways to achieve that goal. My view of women, my understanding of sex, and my approach to life was centered on me and the pleasure I could receive. My thoughts led me down darkened and dangerous paths, taking me in directions I should never have gone, and bringing about choices I should never have made. I ended up doing things I never thought in a million years I would do. It all began with an uncontrolled, undisciplined, unfocused, self-centered mind.

Let me repeat this critical point: What we think will become what we do. If we are going to live daily lives that glorify God, we need to think thoughts that glorify God (Col. 3:2) —not just on occasion or frequently, but moment-by-moment every second of our life (Phil. 4:8). This is why we are to "take captive every thought to make it obedient to Christ" (2 Cor. 10:5). And how do we take our thoughts captive? By using "the sword of the Spirit, which is the word of God" (Eph. 6:17 ESV).

In Psalm 119:105 David declared, "Your word is a lamp to my feet and a light to my path" (ESV). Reading God's Word daily, memorizing Scripture, and thinking throughout my day about what God is saying acts as a flood light on an otherwise shadowy and obscure path. Scripture presents me with the amazing truth of who God is and the humbling reality of what I am. It shows me where my thinking is muddled and wrong. It takes my mind off of Prince-Me and puts it squarely on King Jesus.

In fact, God's Word is "living and active, sharper than any two-edged sword, piercing to the division of soul and of spirit, of joints and of marrow, and discerning the thoughts and intentions of the heart" (Heb. 4:12 ESV; cp. 2 Tim. 3:16-17).

By fixing my eyes (and mind) squarely on Scripture, I was no longer put to shame by my lustful, sexual impurity (Psa. 119:6). I was (and praise God, still am) keeping my way pure by guarding it according to God's Word (Psa. 119:9; Prov. 4:23). Not only did I read my Bible every day, I memorized what I read. As I continue to hide God's Word in my heart (Psa. 119:11), and intentionally walk in obedience to His Truth (Psa. 119:9), I am able to live a sexually pure life today, and so can you.

The Scriptures contained in this devotional guide aren't randomly selected verses to fill a page. Each day's comments aren't just words to make the book bigger. These are the verses God used (and still uses) in my life to get my mind off self and focused on Him. Many of these verses are ones that Roger had me memorize; today I use them every time the Tempter tries to take me down. The comments you read each day are meant to provide that "sense of direction" you may need as you consider the Scripture presented.

AN OUNCE OF PREVENTION

At the end of each week you will see a section entitled "Authentic Accountability." We cannot—we must not—fight this battle alone. God created us (and expects us) to be accountable. You may be familiar with the words of Proverbs 27:17 which say, "As iron sharpens iron, so one man sharpens another." Sounds great, but what does it really mean?

I mentioned earlier that God brought Roger into my life for a purpose. Roger "sharpened" me by making sure I was reading, studying, and memorizing Scripture. He wouldn't accept my flimsy excuses for why I wasn't in the Word that week. He didn't back down when I tried to dance around the fact that I wasn't walking in obedience to what God was teaching me.

The "iron" of his pointed questions struck hard against the iron of my pride. Sometimes the sparks flew. Slowly but surely the rough edges began to come off and a beautiful, polished finish that reflected the Father shone through. I am convinced that God has a "Roger" for you as well.

"Is it really necessary to have an accountability partner as I work through this devotional guide?" You might ask. "Can't I just do these devotions on my own?" Certainly, you can. And I'm sure that if you do, you will receive both a challenge and blessing from it. I can also state with certainty that you will not know the power and strength that an accountability partner can bring to the equation.

I want to strongly encourage you to work through this devotional guide with at least one other person. Meet together weekly—in person, over the phone, Skype, Face Time or use two tin cups and a string, I don't care—but talk through the questions, discuss the devotional theme for that week, pick a verse or two to memorize, pray for and with each other, and be intentional.

A NOTE TO WOMEN

For the ladies who read this book, I want to acknowledge the fact that you too are in the thick of this battle. The pull of lust and sexual desires are not just a man-thing. I know that you are facing this same beast and it can be intimidating and terrifying. It can also be lonely.

The devotions in this book apply to women just as much as they do to men. As I put pen to paper (actually fingers to keyboard), please understand that I am writing to you as well even though I will usually refer to the male gender. Please do not take offense at this, as none is intended.

MY PRAYER

Father, we are Your children longing for victory in our lives. No longer do we want to give in to the temptations that sexual impurity brings. We desire to stand up and stand out, and say, "No more!" And yet, we recognize and acknowledge that we've tried in the past and have horribly failed. We can't do this alone. We need You—and we need each other.

Right now we want to echo the words of David when he said, "Guide [us] in your truth and teach [us], for you are God [our] Savior, and [our] hope is in you all day long" (Psa. 25:5). Lord, You are good and upright. We still battle with sin every day, please instruct us in Your ways as we open this book and study Your Word (Psa. 25:8).

As we work our way through each day's devotion, help us to gain understanding so that we will hate every wrong path (Psa. 119:104), and only—always—walk the path of purity (Psa. 119:9). We so desperately need to hear Your voice behind us saying, "This is the way, walk in it" (Isa. 30:21).

Thank you, Father, for what You are going to accomplish in our lives through Your Spirit's application of Your Word as we go through this study. Amen!

In Christian Brotherhood,

Steve

How to Work Through This Book

Let's take just a moment to familiarize you with the format and layout of this devotional guide.

The Purpose

First, please understand its purpose is not to get you to "do devotions." I want more than that for you. Any of us can do devotions easily enough. Just pick up a devotional book, read the few verses at the top of the page, then glance at the writers comments, say the closing prayer (or read the final poem or quote) and voila—devotions are done for the day. Check that off your list and move on to the next task.

What has that accomplished? Maybe the writer got you to think. Maybe you will even remember that devotional for a few days. You might choose to pass it on to a family member or friend who "needs" it. But did it make lasting change in *your* heart and behavior?

Let's be honest: most of you have done devotions in the past, but you're still struggling with this sin issue in your life. More than likely it's because "you know neither the Scriptures nor the power of God" (Matt. 22:29) which can give you the freedom and victory you so desperately seek.

Now I do not intend that last statement to be offensive. However, I do want it to make you stop and think. Do you truly *know* the Scripture? Are you experiencing God's power in your life? You see, God's Word is perfect, it is also sure, right, pure, clean and highly desirable (Psa. 19:7-10). As you study it, it revives your soul, makes you wise, rejoices your heart, enlightens your eyes, and greatly rewards you (Psa. 19:7-10). To realize victory over lust, porn, masturbation and any other forms of sexual impurity in your life, you must be in God's Word daily!

To that end it's important to understand that this book is not intended to be just another devotional book. It is my deepest desire and passion to help you know real and lasting victory in your life as I have. This is why I have called this "The Pure Man's Devotional GUIDE." The intent of this book is to guide you into and through Scripture.

The Process
This devotional guide is based upon a 7-day week format, beginning on Sunday and ending on Saturday every week for the next five weeks. Plan on investing 20 to 30 minutes daily on every devotional. If you "zip through it" you will not fully benefit from all it has to offer.

1. Each day opens with an intentional prayer point. Do not skip over this in the interest of time. This is an important component to your devotions. Talk with God before diving in. There are specific things you are to ask Him before beginning the devotional of the day.

   Let me give you a word of warning though. After a while it will seem repetitious and you will be tempted to bypass it because "I already know this, and I've done it every single day." Good! This needs to become a habit. The Scripture prayer is one to be memorized and prayed from your heart daily.

2. Each day you will read a specific text from God's Word. What comes after that is not just a personal commentary. You will see more Scripture. I urge you to make the time to open your Bible and read each passage. Ask God to show Himself to you in a mighty way. Have a pad and pen next to you to journal about what you're learning. That notebook will become precious to you.

3. I suggest setting aside a specific time each day to do this study. Try to make it the same time each and every day. I strongly suggest first thing in the morning as it will help you get focused for your day. Develop a habit. Be diligent in protecting that time. Don't let other things get in the way and crowd out this time with God. It's important to stay consistent. Remember, Satan doesn't want you doing this, so he will throw everything in his arsenal at you to keep you from God's Word.

4. Understand that this study will be intense at times. This is because we are addressing an intense problem. Make sure you are alone, in a quiet spot, and able to focus. Have your Bible next to you. Look up the verses and read them out loud if possible. Use the space at the end of each devotional to write down the things that God is speaking to you about. This is so you won't forget later, when the busy-ness of the day takes over. It also enables you to talk with your accountability partner at the end of the week about what God has been teaching you.

5. Don't try to do this on your own. Work through this devotional guide with another person (or persons) of the same gender. There is great power as you read and apply God's Word to your heart. There is also a tremendous sense of hope as you have someone helping you work out your salvation with fear and trembling (Phil. 2:12). Although it certainly can be used as such, please don't use this book as a self-help tool. Don't try to go it alone.

6. At the end of each devotion I want you to take above five minutes to review and assess. What did you just learn? What is God revealing to you and what do you need to do about it? Write it down, then pray about it and commit your action to the Lord. Don't put it off thinking you'll get to that part later. "Later" has a funny way of never showing up.

7. Finally, get together with your accountability partner *weekly* to talk about what you have learned, what you need to do and how you are going to do it. Pray together and watch God work!

WEEK ONE
The Great Motivator

As we begin this week's study, it is important that we take a few moments to talk about motivation—specifically, your motivation. Why do you do the things you do and make the choices you make?

Almost everything we do has a driving force behind it. You eat because you're hungry; you sleep because you're tired; you bite your fingernails because you're anxious about something; and so on. Even our sinful choices have a motive behind them.

So ask yourself this question: Do I *want* to experience real victory in my life? That question may seem to be so fundamentally basic that you wonder why it even needs to be asked. After all, you're reading this book so of course you want victory. And yet, I ask again: Do you —with all your heart—want to be victorious? Before you off-handedly answer, "Well, of course I do," I encourage you to second-guess yourself (maybe even third- and fourth-guess, as well).

For many years I thought I wanted victory in my life. I was under the impression that my deepest desire was to be free from the vice-grip that lust, pornography, and self-gratification (masturbation) had on me. Yet my actions and life-choices said otherwise. Don't take me wrong, the "desire" for it was definitely there, but I was enjoying the perceived pleasures of my sin (Heb. 11:25) way too much to take it any further. There was still a part of me that just didn't want to let it go. I didn't want the victory more than I wanted the war. So the battle raged on.

Real, lasting victory would remain elusive until I reached the point of no return. Until it was do or die, all of my efforts at change were only half-hearted. I wasn't "all in." As a result, I experienced ongoing defeat and discouragement instead of a life of victory and joy. So, again I ask: Do you want, do you truly long—even ache deep in your heart—for genuine, life-changing victory, no matter the cost?

A second question to consider is this: *What* do I want to be victorious from? What needs to change in your life? As long as our struggles and issues remain vague and nameless, we don't know exactly what it is we're up against. When you don't know what you're fighting, you don't know how to combat it. We end up taking potshots in the dark, swinging aimlessly at nothing but air, and hoping against all hope that maybe, just maybe we might connect and strike a blow. So again I ask: What specifically do you want to change in your life? *From what* are you seeking victory?

The final question I want you to consider is this: *Why* do I want to be victorious? What are your real reasons for wanting this victory? Your honest answer to this question will reveal much. You see, it is upon this groundwork that you are building all your efforts and hopes for victory. Your answer to this question determines your success or failure. When we build on the right foundation, we are guaranteed victory. Build on a wrong foundation and we are assured of failure after failure, defeat after defeat.

To experience real change then, we need to take a close, long, hard, and introspective look. If you were candid and sincere in your answers to these questions, you are beginning to catch a glimpse of your heart. This week we are going to explore this topic and dig into the real motivations of your heart. Hang on because here we go!

SUNDAY – A PURE HEART = A PURE MAN
Prayer Time:
As you begin today's devotional, take a moment right now and ask God to reveal Himself to you and to soften your heart to receive what He wants to tell you. Ask Him to give you the strength to apply what you discover to your life—right here and right now.

Father, please fill me right now with the knowledge of Your will in all spiritual wisdom and understanding so that I will walk throughout the day in a manner worthy of You, pleasing You in all respects, bearing fruit for You in everything I do, and increasing in my knowledge of You (Col. 1:10).

"Create in me a clean heart, O God, and renew a right spirit within me." Psalm 51:10 (ESV)

Being a Pure Man isn't just about doing (or not doing) certain things. In other words: not looking at pornography, not having sex with someone other than my wife, not lusting after women at the beach, and not masturbating does not make me a pure man. By the same token, going to church, reading my Bible, singing in the choir, and teaching the fifth-grade Sunday School class at my Church does not make me a Pure Man. Those things can certainly give evidence to purity, but they cannot define it.

Genuine purity begins in the heart. It starts as an attitude, not an action. As King David was contemplating the holiness of God, he was gripped by the question: Who could possibly be allowed into His presence? His conclusion was absolute: Only the one who has clean hands and a pure heart (Psa. 24:3-4). David understood that to be accepted by God, he had to be a Pure Man, and to be a Pure Man he first had to have a pure heart (Prov. 27:19).

He also acknowledged that, because he struggled with a heart that was impure, He needed God to intervene. Look again at our verse for today. David's deep desire was to have a clean heart before God, and he recognized that only God could clean it. You see, without Christ, our heart is deceitful and wicked (Jer. 17:9). Since the fall of man (Gen. 3), "every intention of the thoughts of his heart was only evil continually" (Gen. 6:5 ESV). In other words, left to ourselves, every plan, every purpose we frame in our mind, everything we determine to do will always be displeasing to God because it is in total opposition to what He wants for us.

Open your Bible and read the following verses: Romans 1:28-31 and 3:10-19; Psalm 14:1-3 and 53:2; Ecclesiastes 9:3; Matthew 15:19; Mark 7:21-23 and Jeremiah 4:14. That's some pretty potent stuff! Now let's make this as down-to-earth-practical as we possibly can. Understanding that what we think in our hearts becomes what we do with our lives, what does this indicate your *life* is like without Christ?

Can you begin to grasp why David asks God to "create" in him a pure heart? He understood that outside of God's direct intervention in his life, his heart would be only evil all the time, which meant that his actions would be as well. So his deepest desire was for God to fashion in him a heart that would always focus upon the Almighty. A pure heart.

The fact is, without Christ in your life, you will always make the wrong choices (Jn. 3:19; cp. Psa. 10:4; 53:1-3; Rom. 1:18-32)? No matter how hard you may try, outside of Christ you can never be a Pure Man because you have an impure heart. It is impossible for that which is already dirty (Isa. 64:6; cp. Psa. 51:5) to make that which is dirty, clean (Job 14:4). Dirt can never clean up dirt; it just spreads the dirt around, moving it to other places. We need a holy God to fashion for us a pure heart, removing the old and putting in the new.

Here's the great news: He already has! When Christ shed His blood for us on the cross, that blood washed (purified) us from all of our sin (1 Jn. 1:7; cp. Eph. 1:7; Heb. 9:14; 1 Pet. 1:18-19). Paul writes that anyone who is in Christ is a new creation (2 Cor.5:17). God didn't take your filthy, sin-stained heart and refurbish it; He crucified the old (Gal. 2:20; 2 Cor. 5:17) and gave you a brand-spanking-new one in its place (Ezek. 11:19; 36:26-27; Jer. 24:7). That heart He gave you has been "created to be like God in true righteousness and holiness" (Eph. 4:24). In other words, it's a holy and pure heart!

As we wrap up our thoughts for today, I want to ask a very important, life-changing question. Have you put your faith in Jesus Christ for your salvation? If your answer is anything but "yes," I challenge you to follow-up with an answer to this question: Why not?

Do you understand and accept the fact that you are a sinner (Rom. 3:23; cp. Eccl. 7:20)? God says that because of our sin, we are without excuse before Him (Rom. 1:20; Rom. 2:1-16). We cannot wash away the filth that is in our heart, because we are already filthy. Man cannot save himself no matter how good he tries to be (Tit. 3:5; cp. Rom. 3:20; Gal. 2:16; Eph. 2:8). To make matters even more desperate, because of our sin we deserve to spend all of eternity in the agonizing fires of Hell itself (Rom. 5:12; 6:23a; cp. Ezek. 18:4, 20).

The amazing, fantastic fact is that Jesus Christ loves *you* so much that He paid the horrible price for your sin so that you wouldn't have to (1 Pet. 2:24; cp. Gal. 3:13; Heb. 7:25-27). The only thing you have to do —all that is required of you—to guarantee your place in Heaven for eternity is choose to believe the fact that Jesus died, was buried, and rose again (1 Thess. 4:14; cp. Ac. 16:31; Rom. 10:9; Eph. 2:8-9; 1 Jn. 5:1, 13). He paid it all for you (Jn. 3:16-18; cp. Rom. 3:24-26; 8:3-4; Gal. 3:13; Titus 2:14; Heb. 9:12; 1 Pet. 2:18-21, 24). We cannot earn our way to Heaven; we can, however, accept the free gift of salvation that Christ offers.

So let me encourage you. If you've never cried out to God for forgiveness and acknowledged the fact that He loved you so much He died in your place to pay for your sin, and that He's alive today to give you eternal life, take a moment right now and talk to Him.

Review, Assess, and Pray:
In the space below, answer the questions. Then, invest at least five minutes in prayer. Tell God your fears and struggles. Ask Him to open your heart and give you His strength to apply what you learned today to your life.

1) What did I learn from this?

2) What does God want me to do about it?

MONDAY – HIDE OR SEEK
Prayer Time:
Before you begin today's devotional, take a moment right now and ask God to reveal Himself to you in a powerful way. Ask Him to soften your heart so that you can receive what He wants to tell you. Ask Him to give you the strength to apply it to your life.

Father, please fill me right now with the knowledge of Your will in all spiritual wisdom and understanding so that I will walk throughout the day in a manner worthy of You, pleasing You in all respects, bearing fruit for You in everything I do, and increasing in my knowledge of You (Col. 1:9-10).

"The LORD does not look at the things man looks at. Man looks at the outward appearance, but the Lord looks at the heart" 1 Samuel 16:7

It is our heart that reveals what is most important to us, and our heart dictates our actions (Prov. 27:19). You see, "as [a man] thinketh in his heart, so is he" (Prov. 23:7 KJV). My friend, I can't emphasize enough the fact that your heart is what matters most to God.   Just take a moment to re-read and think about today's verse.

The things that impress us do not impress God. We may take note of a persons' dress, stature, and demeanor. We might be impressed with their knowledge of Scripture, ability to lead in worship, or charismatic presence on the platform. We may even appreciate their service in the nursery, or volunteering to clean the toilets in the children's department.   However, God isn't excited about those things if the motive of their heart is wrong.

I was a pastor for 12 years.   I stood behind the pulpit every Sunday and taught from the Word of God.   People got saved; people committed their lives to God. I counseled on how to deal with sin issues and some individuals even experienced real change. I married couples and buried church members. People were impressed with my ministry—and yet all of that was a front, a fake, and a farce.

I "looked beautiful on the outside but on the inside (I was) full of dead men's bones and everything unclean" (this was Christ's definition of the Pharisees in Matt. 23:27). Inside I was a porn addict and adulterer (Matt. 5:28).   In my heart I lusted after other women. I may have impressed others, but God knew better.   Our heart exposes what is most important to us. So what is your heart revealing?

Psalm 44:21 says, God "knows the secrets of the heart."   You can't play hide-or-seek with God. He can see clearly into every nook and cranny of your life and fully recognize everything that's there.

Furthermore, He knows even the dark "secrets" of your heart. He has searched you and knows "when (you) sit and when (you) rise," He perceives your thoughts from afar and discerns your "going out and (your) lying down." He is "familiar with all (your) ways" (Psa. 139:1-4).

The bottom line is actually quite simple. "There is no dark place, no deep shadow where (we) can hide" (Job 34:22). No one—let me repeat this so that it's very clear—no one can "hide in secret places so that (God) cannot see him" (Jer. 23:24). God knows all the secrets of your heart.

Why do you think the thoughts you think and do the things you do? "All a man's ways seem right to him, but the LORD weighs the heart" (Prov. 21:2). We make our choices and decisions because we believe they are the right ones. We walk down a particular path in life because we think it's the correct way to go. We believe that is what will make us happy, and we're convinced that is where we will find fulfillment and pleasure.

I used to justify my sinful choices by using the rest of humanity as my excuse. Oh sure, I would admit I was a sinner, but would also let myself off the hook because "I'm not as bad as So-n-So" and, "Well, at least *I'm* not doing that!" "In (my) own eyes (I) flattered (myself) too much to detect or hate (my) sin" (Psa. 36:2 addition mine).

Remember—always remember—God looks at the heart. "You ... justify yourselves in the eyes of men, but God knows your hearts. What is highly valued among men is detestable in God's sight" (Lk. 16:15). He looks past the excuses and puts the motives of your heart on the scales (Proverbs 16:2). You can make every excuse in the book (and even write some of your own), but "Does not he who weighs the heart perceive it? Does not he who guards your life know it? Will he not repay each person according to what he has done" (Prov. 24:12)?

As long as your reason for fighting this battle is self-focused—as long as your motivations for breaking free from impurity are centered on the things you want for your life, victory will be elusive. Always *almost* within your grasp, but never quite there.

7

Review, Assess, and Pray:
In the space below, answer the questions. Then, invest at least five minutes in prayer. Tell God your fears and struggles. Ask Him to open your heart and give you His strength to apply what you learned today to your life.

    1) What did I learn from this?

    2) What does God want me to do about it?

TUESDAY – ARE YOU ALL IN?

Prayer Time:
Don't lose sight of the fact that this opening prayer time is an important part of each day's devotional. Don't skip it. Take a moment right now and ask God to reveal Himself to you in a powerful way, to soften your heart to receive what He wants to tell you, and to give you the understanding, wisdom, and strength to apply it to your life.

Father, I desperately need the knowledge of Your will in all spiritual wisdom and understanding, only then will I walk in a manner worthy of You, pleasing You in all respects, bearing fruit for You in everything I do, and increasing in my knowledge of You (Col. 1:10).

———————

"Whether you eat or drink or whatever you do, do it all for the glory of God." 1 Corinthians 10:31

What reason should we have for wanting a victory that will help us actually win the war against sexual impurity and put that ol' dragon down? The first thing we need to address is that it's not about you! It's not about *you* having victory, or about *you* winning the war, or even about *you* being pure. Read our verse for the day again. My friend, we will never be successful in finding freedom from our struggles with impurity until our primary reason for wanting it is so that our victory and ongoing purity will glorify God.

As long as it is about us, then we will snatch the glory for our self when the battle is over. "Look what I did! Look at all that my hard work accomplished! I deserve this victory!" That is precisely what God wants us to avoid.

A great example of this is found in the book of Judges where we read of a man named Gideon. Leading an army of nearly 32,000 men, he's about to charge the camp of the Midianites—a formidable army of 135,000. Early in the morning, as Gideon stands outside his tent surveying the camp, God approaches Gideon and tells him he has too many men and that he needs to begin the process of whittling down his army until he is left with only 300 men. Talk about poor odds.

Why did God do that? What was His purpose? If we could have listened in to His conversation with Gideon, I wonder if we would have heard something like this: "Gideon." "Yes, my Lord." "Gideon, you have too many men for me to deliver Midian into their hands." Gideon chuckles; a little surprised that God would show His sense of humor at a moment like this. Silence.

Nervously clearing his throat, Gideon says: "Umm, Lord? Would you mind repeating that last order?" "Yes, Gideon, you have too many men for me to deliver Midian into their hands. I want you to get rid of the majority of your army." Gideon tries not to look surprised. The men were already worried about being outnumbered as it is, and rightly so. They would surely doubt his ability to lead such a battle if he sent even a fraction of them home. "May I be so bold as to ask why, my Lord?" "You are to decrease your numbers in order that Israel may not boast against Me that her *own* strength has saved her" (see Judg. 7:2).

Did you catch that? God intentionally shrunk the size of Gideon's army because He didn't want Israel claiming glory for themselves after they had won the battle. He knew that man struggles with pride. He knew that the men would look at their handiwork and accept responsibility for the victory. Never forget that God will always work only for His own glory. If God is going to help you fight against the beast of impurity and win, it must be on His terms and for His glory, or He will not help you (Col. 3:17; cp. 1 Thess. 4:1; Prov. 25:27).

It is said of King Hezekiah, "In everything that he undertook ... he sought His God and worked wholeheartedly. And so he prospered" (2 Chron. 31:21). Now, prospering sounds like a good thing doesn't it? The word here literally refers to enjoying great success. I'm pretty sure I am safe in saying that you would like to enjoy great success in this battle against lust, pornography, and masturbation.

Listen closely, my friend: In everything you undertake, in every aspect of this war, you must seek God's strength, God's wisdom, and God's glory. Only then will you prosper. When it seems that you can't win this battle, when you feel totally surrounded and pressed in upon to the point that defeat is imminent, that's a good thing. That means you understand you can't win. Seek God with your whole heart. It is only through Him that you will find the strength to fight (Phil 4:13). Only He will provide the victory.

In 2 Kings 6 the king of Syria sends "horses and chariots and a great army" by night to surround the prophet Elisha (2 Ki. 6:14 ESV). In the morning Elisha's servant:

> Rose early in the morning and went out, behold, an army with horses and chariots was all around the city. And the servant said 'Alas, my master! What shall we do?' He said, 'Do not be afraid, for those who are with us are more than those who are with them.' Then Elisha prayed and said, 'O LORD, please open his eyes that he may see.' So the LORD opened the eyes of the young man, and he saw, and behold, the mountain was full of horses and chariots of fire all around Elisha. (2 Ki. 6:15-17 ESV)

The God of Elisha is our God! The God who surrounded His servant surrounds you. The God who stood ready to help, stands ready to help you! What a great and glorious promise!

Review, Assess, and Pray:
In the space below, answer the questions. Then, invest at least five minutes in prayer. Tell God your fears and struggles. Ask Him to open your heart and give you His strength to apply what you learned today to your life.

1) What did I learn from this?

2) What does God want me to do about it?

WEDNESDAY – FOR GOD AND GOD ALONE

Prayer Time:
Please take a moment right here and now to ask God to reveal Himself to you. Ask Him to soften your heart so you may receive what He wants to tell you, and to give you the strength to apply it to your life.

Father, You are hitting me hard this week and it's only Wednesday! Thank you. Please fill me with the knowledge of Your will in all spiritual wisdom and understanding so that I will walk today in a manner worthy of You, pleasing You in all respects, bearing fruit for You in everything I do, and increasing in my knowledge of You (Col. 1:10).

———————————

"I am the LORD; that is my name; my glory I give to no other, nor my praise to carved idols." Isaiah 42:8 (ESV)

In 2 Chronicles we see that King Uzziah "did what was right in the eyes of the LORD ... as long as he sought the LORD, God gave him success" (2 Chron. 26:4-5). I assure you my friend, victory is possible! And when you seek freedom from impurity for the purpose of bringing honor and glory to God, He promises to give you "rest on every side" (2 Chron. 14:7). Understand that this is not a promise that you will no longer be tempted. It is, however, an assurance that you don't have to give in to the temptation!

So I'd say the correct answer to the question we've been asking this week—"What's your motivation?"—should be pretty clear. The motivation that God will honor is to "devote (my) heart and soul to

11

seeking the LORD (my) God" (1 Chron. 22:19; cp. Matt. 6:33) for the sole purpose of bringing Him honor, glory, and praise.

Allow me to repeat this point: We *must* have God's glory as our primary motivation for victory over, and freedom from sexual impurity. When my ultimate goal is to feel better about myself or to save my marriage, I am actually guilty of placing "King Me" on the throne of my heart in place of God. When I pursue anything but God, I make myself, my goals, my desires, and my wants—even my fears— a "god" in my life. What I worship is what I will serve, and God is very clear that serving anything or anyone other than Him is unacceptable (Exod. 20:3; Deut. 5:7; 6:5, 14; Josh. 24:23).

When you are able to effectively say "No" to the sinful desires of the flesh, it's only because God has given you the strength to do so. Every time you turn your eyes away from that temptation and focus your mind on things that are true, noble, right, pure, lovely, and admirable (Phil. 4:8), it's only because God has provided you with His divine power (2 Peter 1:3) to take His way of escape (1 Cor. 10:13). Permanent freedom from impurity brings glory to God.

God stands ready to help. He wants you to live in victory and freedom. But He also wants to be the One who gets the glory. Your freedom is an incredible opportunity to give honor and praise to the One who actually set you free. There is one thing, and only one thing that you and I can do to know this victory. Are you ready to hear it? We must fully surrender our heart and mind over to the One who loves us so deeply that He died for us. That's it. Surrender yourself completely to Him and trust Him to change your heart.

Then, as you share your testimony of victory with men, you will not be boasting in yourself. A story of victory must never be a "here's what I was, and look at what I've become" kind of tale. We should be deeply ashamed of the wicked things we have done. We should be humiliated (and mortified) at the man we have turned into and the pain we have caused so many people. No, this must never be a boast about you. Rather, this is about God and all HE has done in our life.

I love the words of Isaiah 61:1.

The Spirit of the Sovereign Lord is on me, because the Lord has anointed me to preach good news to the poor. He has sent me to bind up the brokenhearted, to proclaim freedom for the captives *(to those battling against lust, pornography, and masturbation)* and release from darkness for the prisoners." (addition mine)

What I'm about to say to you comes from the bottom of my heart: I want you to be a pure man. I want you to boast in what God is doing in your life. God says the pure man will always "boast about this: that he understands and knows (God), that (He is) the Lord, who exercises kindness, justice and righteousness on earth" (Jer. 9:24). That is what delights the Lord. That is what glorifies God. That is why He will help you know victory.

God promises freedom to those who walk with Him, looking to Him for guidance and power. David said with confidence, "I will walk about in freedom, for I have sought out your precepts" (Psa. 119:45). Believe me, God wants you to be free. In fact, "It is for freedom that Christ has set us free. Stand firm, then, and do not let yourselves be burdened again by a yoke of slavery" (Gal. 5:1).

Review, Assess, and Pray:
In the space below, answer the questions. Then, invest at least five minutes in prayer. Tell God your fears and struggles. Ask Him to open your heart and give you His strength to apply what you learned today to your life.

    1) What did I learn from this?

    2) What does God want me to do about it?

THURSDAY – THE DETHRONING OF KING ME
Prayer Time:
You're doing great! Keep up the great work and pause for just a moment to ask God to reveal Himself to you today, and to soften your heart so that you can receive what He wants to tell you. Then ask

Him to give you the strength to apply to your life what you learn today.

Father, as I am seeking You, please fill me with the knowledge of Your will in all spiritual wisdom and understanding so that I will walk today in a manner worthy of You, pleasing You in all respects, bearing fruit for You in everything I do, and increasing in my knowledge of You (Col. 1:10).

"Not to (me), O LORD, not to (me) but to your name give glory, for the sake of your steadfast love and your faithfulness." Psalm 115:1 (ESV)

Listen, my friend, there is great joy "in (God's) strength. How great is (our) joy in the victories (God) gives" (Psa. 21:1). Your success over this three-headed dragon totally "depends on God; he is (your) mighty rock, (your) refuge" (Psa. 62:7). To know real and lasting victory, you need to cry out, "Help (me), O God (my) Savior, for the glory of your name; deliver (me) and forgive (my sin) for your name's sake" (Psa. 79:9). "For the sake of your name, O LORD, forgive my iniquity, though it is great" (Psa. 25:11).

I would like to once again ask you this all-important question: What is your real motive for finding freedom from bondage to impurity? Are you discovering that you have been engaged in this battle with the wrong intent and for the wrong reasons? Can you begin to understand why you've been losing this battle? Can you see how important it is that your motivation is to honor and glorify God in everything, including this war? I challenge you to make today's verse the cry of your heart.

Do you know what time it is? No, I'm not referring to the clock on your wall or the watch on your wrist. I'm talking about this specific time in your life. I'm talking about today, right here, right now. We desperately need to understand "the present time. The hour has come for (us) to wake up from (our) slumber, because our salvation is nearer now than when we first believed" (Rom. 13:11).

I am laying the gauntlet down before you. I challenge you to "come back to your senses as you ought, and stop sinning" (1 Cor. 15:34). I

14

dare you to "not be like others, who are asleep, but ... be alert and self-controlled" (1 Thess. 5:6). I urge you, "whether you eat, or drink, or whatever you do, do it all for the glory of God" (1 Cor. 10:31). And I assure you, with God as your focus, with the glory of God as the goal of your heart, you can place your foot on the head of that slain dragon and cry out, "I have fought the good fight, I have finished the race, I have kept the faith" (2 Tim. 4:7).

I feel strongly led at this moment to pray Scripture for you. I realize I probably don't know you, and I definitely don't know everything that is going on in your life. But our Father does, and He stands ready to help you know real and lasting victory. Here is my prayer for you:

> "May the LORD answer you when you are in distress; may the name of the God of Jacob protect you. May he send you help from the sanctuary and grant you support from Zion. May he remember all your sacrifices and accept your burnt offerings. May he give you the desire of your heart and make all your plans succeed" (Psa. 20:1-4).

Now I have a favor to ask of you. As you begin to experience real victory in your life, and as you begin to give God the glory for what He is doing in your heart, would you please let me know? You can go to our website (www.thepureman.org) for information on how to either write me an email or call me. I want to rejoice with you over what God is accomplishing in your life. I want to "shout for joy when you are victorious and lift up our banners in the name of our God. May the LORD grant all your requests" (Psa. 20:5).

Review, Assess, and Pray:
In the space below, answer the questions. Then, invest five minutes in prayer. Tell God your fears and struggles. Ask Him to open your heart and give you His strength to apply His truth to your life.

1) What did I learn from this?

2) What does God want me to do about it?

FRIDAY – KEEPING PERSPECTIVE

Prayer Time:

Take a moment before you begin today and ask God to open your eyes to His Truth. Ask Him to soften your heart so that you can receive what He wants to tell you, and to give you the strength to apply it to your life.

Father, as I read today's devotional, please help me understand that You are for my life. I want to walk today in a manner worthy of You, pleasing You in all respects, bearing fruit for You in everything I do, and increasing in my knowledge of You (Col. 1:10).

"Know that the Lord, he is God! It is he who made us, and we are his; we are his people, and the sheep of his pasture." Psalm 100:3 (ESV)

Picture this: It's Sunday morning. You're at church and the worship service has begun. The music begins and everyone joins in singing. Those around you have heads bowed while others have hands lifted high. Corporately the words of the song ring out, "In my life, Lord, be glorified; be glorified. In my life, Lord, be glorified today!"

This week we've been talking about the motivation of our heart. We've learned that it must be for God's glory or we will not know real victory in our battle against sexual impurity. Read today's verse again. True purpose and meaning to life is found only when we are doing that which God created us to do: living a godly life that brings honor and glory to Him (1 Cor. 10:31; cp. Col. 3:17; Eccl 12:13).

In the book of Ecclesiastes we read the story of a man named Solomon who embarks on this massive quest to find purpose and meaning for his life. He tries to find satisfaction and fulfillment in money, possessions, relationships, and pleasures—he runs the whole gambit. Yet, no matter how hard he tried, how much money he put in the bank, how many things he accumulated, how many friendships he developed, or how many different types of pleasures he pursued, he just could not find happiness (Read Eccl. 1-2).

Aren't we in the same boat? How many times have you pursued lust, porn, masturbation, and other forms of sexual impurity? How desperately did you want those things to satisfy you and fill that emptiness inside? How successful were you? True satisfaction comes only when we fulfill the intent of our Creator. Meaning, purpose, happiness, and joy come only when we discover an intimate and personal relationship with God and walk in total obedience to His commands.

> "What does the Lord your God require of you, but to fear the Lord your God, to walk in all his ways, to love him, to serve the Lord your God with all your heart and with all your soul, and to keep the commandments and statutes of the Lord, which I am commanding you today for your good?" (Deut. 10:12-13 ESV; cp. 1 Sam. 15:22; Prov. 21:3; Mark 12:29-31).

I don't think God could make it any clearer. A life lived in pursuit of bringing glory to Him is where we will find victory.

By the way, Solomon learned a valuable lesson from his failed attempts. Nothing, absolutely nothing but God can bring you true joy, happiness, meaning, fulfillment, and satisfaction in life. So the main thing in life should be to "fear God and keep His commandments" (Eccl. 12:13). Are you keeping the main thing the main thing?

As we head into the weekend, let me encourage you that victory over sexual impurity isn't a pipe dream; it's possible! We do not have to live defeated lives. For years I focused all my attention on changing outwardly, trying to behave the way I thought I knew God wanted me to. I believed that making those changes would bring me happiness and that long-sought-after victory. The problem was that the motivation of my heart was all about me.

During that time of my life I struggled with feelings of failure, defeat, and discouragement. No more! This sin that we battle with is not greater than God (1 Jn. 4:4). The temptations that seemingly overwhelm you are actually powerless over you. You *can* live a consistent, godly life! You can learn how to walk in true victory over sin and to live a life that glorifies our Heavenly Father. Stick with this devotional guide, continue on this journey, and together we'll discover what victory looks and feels like!

Review, Assess, and Pray:
In the space below, answer the questions. Then, invest five minutes in prayer. Tell God your fears and struggles. Ask Him to open your heart and give you His strength to apply His truth to your life.

1) What did I learn from this?

2) What does God want me to do about it?

SATURDAY – FOLLOWING YOUR HEART

Prayer Time:
Take a moment before you begin today and ask God to reveal Himself to you, to soften your heart to receive what He wants to tell you, and to give you the strength to apply it to your life.

Father, fill me with the knowledge of Your will in all spiritual wisdom and understanding so that I will walk today in a manner worthy of You, pleasing You in all respects, bearing fruit for You in everything I do, and increasing in my knowledge of You (Col. 1:9-10).

"For those who live according to the flesh set their minds on the things of the flesh, but those who live according to the Spirit set their minds on the things of the Spirit." Romans 8:5 (ESV)

What is your mind set upon? Where is the focus of your heart? As long as it is on self, you will not succeed. Paul speaks of "those who are self-seeking," and states that they "do not obey the truth, but obey unrighteousness" (Rom. 2:8 ESV). Does that describe the motivation of your heart? Have you been self-seeking? If so, then you shouldn't be surprised at the choices you have been making.

For years I was a Pharisee at heart. I kept the outside of my life looking clean and presentable, even respectable; all the while the inside was full of greed and self-indulgence (Matt. 23:25). When King

Me is sitting on the throne of your heart, you will worship and serve King Me. That is why we fail to glorify God. That is why we struggle with impurity.

The rest of today's devotional is slightly different from the others this week in that I want us to focus all of our attention on Scripture. Please read each verse below, pausing to ask the Holy Spirit to show you where your heart is. Ask Him to reveal to you the real motivations of your heart.

As the Spirit begins to move in you, understand that He is bringing "to light the things now hidden in darkness" and He is disclosing "the purposes of the heart" (1 Cor. 4:5 ESV). What will you do with what He reveals to you? In what ways are you being self-serving, self-centered, and self-focused?

- "Do not store up for yourselves treasures on earth, where moth and rust destroy, and where thieves break in and steal. But store up for yourselves treasures in heaven, where moth and rust do not destroy, and where thieves do not break in and steal. For where your treasure is, there your heart will be also" (Matt. 6:19-21). What are you treasuring?

- "You hypocrites! Isaiah was right when he prophesied about you: These people honor me with their lips, but their hearts are far from me. They worship me in vain; their teachings are but rules taught by men" (Matt. 15:7-9). Is your worship in vain? Where is your heart?

- "Blind Pharisee! First clean the inside of the cup and dish, and then the outside will also be clean" (Matt. 23:26). What, inside of you, needs to be cleaned?

- "And he died for all, that those who live might no longer live for themselves but for him who for their sake died and was raised" (2 Cor. 5:15). Whom are you living for?

- "No one can serve two masters, for either he will hate the one and love the other, or he will be devoted to the one and despise the other" (Matt. 6:24). Are you serving self or God?

Let me remind you what we have learned this week: Man looks on the outward appearance (1 Sam. 16:7)—but in the end it really doesn't matter what man thinks. God looks on your heart (1 Sam. 16:7; cp. Jer. 17:9-10). He sees your real motives and rewards accordingly.

So, why do you want to be free from sexual impurity? If it's for anything other than God's honor and glory, no matter how noble and pure, He will not help. So ask God to test you, try you, and examine your heart and mind (Psa. 26:2). Then, as He reveals to you the secret recesses of your heart, ask Him to

> Teach me your way, O Lord, and I will walk in your truth; give me an undivided heart, that I may fear your name. I will praise you, O Lord my God, with all my heart; I will glorify your name forever. For great is your love toward me; you have delivered me from the depths of the grave. (Psa. 86:11-13)

Review, Assess, and Pray:
In the space below, answer the questions. Then, invest five minutes in prayer. Tell God your fears and struggles. Ask Him to open your heart and give you His strength to apply His truth to your life.

1) What did I learn from this?

2) What does God want me to do about it?

AUTHENTIC ACCOUNTABILITY

At the end of every week you will see this section called Authentic Accountability. Its purpose is two-fold:

First, to allow you to review the past week. What have you learned? What needs to change in your life? What steps are you taking to make those changes?

Second, to create a discussion-point between you and your accountability partner(s). We should never try to overcome sexual impurity on our own. We need one another. We need someone who will meet with us weekly, ask the tough questions, pray with us and for us, be firm with us when needed; in short—hold us accountable.

1. What did you learn from this week's set of devotions?

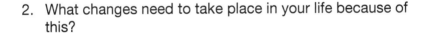

2. What changes need to take place in your life because of this?

3. What steps of faith are you going to take to make those changes?

4. Select at least one verse from this week to memorize. Explain why you chose that verse and how it applies to you.

WEEK TWO
Who's Really In Charge?

You wouldn't believe (...well, actually you probably would) how many times I have tried to climb the hill of victory over lust, porn, masturbation, and all other forms of sexual impurity—reaching almost to the flag at the top of the mountain—only to find myself sliding back down the slippery slope of selfishness because of one stupid decision in a moment of weakness. Are you with me? Can you relate?

Afterward, I would become so discouraged and defeated that I was tempted, on more than one occasion, to just throw in the towel and quit. I would mentally and verbally beat myself up, calling myself an idiot, a fool, and other things that are probably not wise to write here. I would ask God to forgive me, then try to pull myself up by my own proverbial bootstraps, and start climbing the hill again for the umpteenth time—because that's what a good-Christian-guy is supposed to do.

God lovingly and patiently taught me that is not how I will know victory. This week we are going to discover from Scripture that we can't fight this battle on our own, nor should we try. This is because God never intended us to. He commanded Joshua to "Be strong and courageous. Do not be frightened, and do not be dismayed, for the Lord your God is with you wherever you go" (Josh. 1:9 ESV).

Each day, as you dive into God's Word, ask the Holy Spirit to show you where you have tried in your own strength to be free of this beast. Ask Him to help you see that self-reformation doesn't work. It can't, simply because it leaves God out of the equation. Look for God to show you what it means to do all things through His power (Phil. 4:13).

The next time you are facing the dragon and feel weak and helpless, read these verses out loud:

> O God, we have heard with our ears, our fathers have told us the work that **You did** in their days, in the days of old. **You** with **Your own hand** drove out the nations; then **You** planted them; **You** afflicted the peoples, then **You** spread them abroad. For by their own sword they did not possess the land, and their own arm did not save them, but **Your** right hand and **Your** arm and the light of **Your** presence, for **You** favored them. You are my King, O God; command victories for Jacob. **Through You** we will push back our adversaries; **through Your name** we will trample down those who rise up against us. For I will not trust in my bow, nor will my sword save me. But **You** have saved us from our adversaries, and **You** have put to shame those who hate us. (Psa.44:1-7 NASB, emphasis added)

Are you ready to find real, lasting victory? Here we go!

SUNDAY – WHO IS YOUR GOD?
Prayer Time:
This prayer time is so important to these devotionals. I trust you aren't skipping over them to try to save time. We need this.

Take a moment before you begin today's devotional and ask God to reveal Himself to you in a mighty way, not just through this devotional, but also through your worship of Him with other believers at church. Ask Him to soften your heart to receive what He wants to tell you, and to give you the strength to apply it to your life.

Father, please reveal to me where I have tried to win this war in my own strength. Fill me with the knowledge of Your will in all spiritual wisdom and understanding so that I will understand what it means to walk in a manner worthy of You, pleasing You in all respects, bearing fruit for You in everything I do, and increasing in my knowledge of You (Col. 1:10).

"The LORD is my strength and my song, and he has become my salvation; this is my God, and I will praise him, my father's God, and I will exalt him." Exodus 15:2 (ESV)

Today is a day meant to focus all of our attention on God—a day of worship. Many of us will go to church, greet each other with a smile, sing worship songs as a congregation, open our Bible and listen to the preacher deliver his sermon, then shake his hand on the way out the door. But did we really worship? Did we truly honor God from our hearts or did we simply play "church"? Are you a one-day, only-on-Sunday Christian?

Unfortunately, many of us will sit in the pew and go through the motions while feeling numb and empty inside. We can't truly worship because we have unresolved issues and unconfessed sin residing in an unrepentant heart. There is a prodigal in the pew (Luke 15:11-32).

This week we will talk about the fact that we can't fight this battle for purity on our own. We will discover that to win this war, we must be in God's Word every day studying it, memorizing it, meditating on it, and obeying it. Just look at today's verse and let its words sink in.

The Lord is your strength. He alone is your source of power—today, tomorrow, Tuesday through Saturday—and repeat. And, oh, what power He has! "Yours, O Lord, is the greatness and the power and the glory and the victory and the majesty, for all that is in the heavens and in the earth is yours. Yours is the kingdom, O Lord, and you are exalted as head above all" (1 Chron. 29:11 ESV).

Only through Him, only through His might can we stop, once-and-for-all, the rampaging beast of sexual immorality that is running amok in our heart. "The Lord will fight for you, and you have only to be silent" (Exod. 14:14 ESV). As you worship God today, just be still and know that He is God (Psa. 46:10). He is your strength, your shield, and when you fully trust in him, you are victorious (Psa. 28:7).

Read these next verses aloud and listen closely to what you're reading:

- "The LORD is my light and my salvation; whom shall I fear? The Lord is the stronghold of my life; of whom shall I be afraid?" (Psa. 27:1 ESV). When you are in that dark place, and you are battling with temptation, shout out this truth—the Lord is my light! He will show you the way out (1 Cor. 10:13). He is your salvation—He will rescue you if you will let Him. You don't need to fear giving in to sexual impurity because the rock upon which you are building is your stronghold, your fortress, and your refuge.

- "O my Strength, I will sing praises to you, for you, O God, are my fortress, the God who shows me steadfast love" (Psa. 59:17 ESV). When you're standing next to other believers in church next week, you can genuinely worship your Heavenly Father from the bottom of your heart because the God who loves you deeply and unconditionally has given you the strength all week long to fight the beast and win!

So "do not throw away your confidence" when in the midst of the battle, for your faith in Him "has a great reward" (Heb. 10:35 ESV).

Review, Assess, and Pray:
In the space below, answer the questions. Then, invest five minutes in prayer. Tell God your fears and struggles. Ask Him to open your heart and give you His strength to apply His truth to your life.

1) What did I learn from this?

2) What does God want me to do about it?

MONDAY – NEVER GIVE UP, NEVER SURRENDER!
Prayer Time:
This is the beginning of real change in your life. Take a moment before you start today's devotional and ask God to reveal Himself to you in a powerful way. Ask Him to soften your heart so you can

receive what He wants to tell you. Ask Him to show you where you have tried in your own strength to be free of sexual impurity, and then ask Him to give you the strength to apply what you learn from His Word to your life.

Father, fill me with the knowledge of Your will in all spiritual wisdom and understanding so that I will walk today in a manner worthy of You, pleasing You in all respects, bearing fruit for You in everything I do, and increasing in my knowledge of You (Col. 1:10).

"And let us not grow weary of doing good, for in due season we will reap, if we do not give up." Galatians 6:9 ESV

Okay, I'm a bit of a sci-fi fan; I admit it. In 1999 a film came out that was a parody of Star Trek. The movie was about washed-up stars of a fictional TV series called *Galaxy Quest*. In the movie an alien race (the Thermians), who had no concept of fiction, followed the broadcast, thinking it was a "historical document," and modeled every aspect of their society after the show. The actors end up joining the Thermians in an attempt to stop a master villain who is threatening to destroy the aliens. Captain Jason Nesmith (played by actor Tim Allen) had a tagline that stuck with me, hence the title of today's devotional—"Never Give Up, Never Surrender!"

If you're like me, the battle against lust and porn and all forms of sexual impurity can be downright exhausting, even defeating at times. So much so that you find yourself wanting to just give up and give in.

Do you ever just get tired of it all? Have you ever found yourself saying, "I quit! I just can't do this anymore! It's useless to try to fight this beast!"? Oh, my friend, do not grow weary of doing good. Don't give up!

When the apostle Paul wrote about his personal struggles with temptation, he said, "I do not understand my own actions. For I do not do what I want, but I do the very thing I hate" (Rom. 7:15 ESV). Can you relate to that? You want to glorify God with your life, you want to be a godly man, and you want to live victorious over lust and the persistent pull of sexual desire. Instead, you find yourself looking down women's tops, staring at pornographic images, and

27

masturbating while you fantasize—the very things we hate to do, we do!

Paul then goes on to say, "I delight in the law of God in my inner being, but I see in my (body) another law waging war against the law of my mind and making me captive to the law of sin that dwells in my (body). Wretched man that I am! Who will deliver me ...?" (Rom. 7:22-24 ESV, additions mine). Again, can you relate?

Our text today is encouraging us to not quit. When you feel weary, when you are tired of trying and think you're about to give in—don't. God has a plan for you—a plan to bless you, not to harm you (Jer. 29:11). He hasn't forsaken you and He is here with you right now, even though it may not seem like it.

When we quit, we are saying that God has failed us. When we give up, we are saying that we don't trust God to do as He promised. When we abandon the battle, we are saying that God's timetable and way of doing things doesn't match up with our own plans for our life and we think we can do better. This kind of action reveals that we lack faith. When we trust God and His timing, our faith reveals that we "believe that he exists and that he rewards those who seek him" (Heb. 11:6 ESV).

The bottom line is: we can't do it on our own and we can't do better than God. Our failures in the past prove that point loud and clear. The answer is not to just give up and give in. Remember, you can do all things through Christ, because He gives you the strength (Phil. 4:13; cp. 2 Pet. 1:3)!

Memorize today's verse and don't give up. In due season, at a predetermined time known to God, you will receive a beautiful harvest from the purity you've tried so hard to sow by faith.

When you feel the weight of the battle, when your mind is telling you to just toss in the towel and stop fighting it, quote today's verse and then call your accountability partner. Remind yourself that as you are fighting for purity, as you are crawling up that hill inch by painful inch toward the victory flag, you are doing what God has commanded (and enabled) you to do. So "be steadfast, immovable ... knowing that in the Lord your labor is not in vain" (1 Cor. 15:58 ESV).

Review, Assess, and Pray:
In the space below, answer the questions. Then, invest five minutes in prayer. Tell God your fears and struggles. Ask Him to open your heart and give you His strength to apply His truth to your life.

1) What did I learn from this?

2) What does God want me to do about it?

TUESDAY – DO YOUR DUTY, SOLDIER!

Prayer Time:
Welcome back! Thank you for your faithfulness and consistency. I know this may be a struggle for you. I understand that it's rough sometimes to make the time to read this, so I applaud your stick-to-it-iveness!

Take a moment before you begin today to quiet your heart before God and ask His Spirit to guide you into His truth. Ask Him to help you receive what He wants to tell you, and give you the strength to apply it to your life.

Father, fill me with the knowledge of Your will in all spiritual wisdom and understanding so that I will walk today in a manner worthy of You, pleasing You in all respects, bearing fruit for You in everything I do, and increasing in my knowledge of You (Col. 1:10).

_____

"Now all has been heard; here is the conclusion of the matter: Fear God and keep His commandments, for this is the whole duty of man." Ecclesiastes 12:13

In Ecclesiastes 1:14 Solomon says, "I have seen all the things that are done under the sun; all of them are meaningless, a chasing after the wind." A little bit later he states, "Then I considered all that my hands had done and the toil I had expended in doing it, and behold, all was

29

vanity and a striving after wind, and there was nothing to be gained under the sun" (Eccl. 2:11 ESV; cp. Eccl. 2:17, 21; 3:19).

In our battle against lust, porn, and sexual impurity in our life, sometimes (nah, let's be honest—most of the time) we can relate with Solomon. We look at all the effort we've expended in trying to be a pure man, we consider the agony of the battle as we white-knuckle our way through the rough spots and we can become easily discouraged. We feel defeated because, after all that, we still gave in during a weak moment. All that effort, and nothing was gained.

At that instant, as we are engaged in hand-to-hand combat with our enemy (Eph. 6:12), he is whispering his lies into our mind—remember, he is a master liar (Jn. 8:44). "God doesn't love you; God doesn't care about your struggles; God won't help you; what kind of a God is He anyway that He would let you suffer like this. Why try; why fight it; why not give up and give in? You'll feel a whole lot better when you do!"

Consider this: God never expects you to fight this battle on your own. He simply wants you to focus all your attention and energy on two things: keeping His commands and fearing Him (Eccl. 12:13). Those two things comprise the "whole duty of man." When you make your life all about Him, God will help you with everything else (see Matt. 6:33). God just wants you to stand firm in your faith in Him; He will give you the tools and the strength to just say, "NO!"

The reason we experience defeat and discouragement is because we've been trying to win this thing on our own. Oh, we may memorize Scripture, meet regularly with our accountability partners, and read our Bible, but what is the motivation of our heart behind all those things (Matt. 6:1; cp. Gal. 1:10; Prov. 16:2; 21:2; Col. 3:23)? If it's so that you can be victorious over LuPoMas (see the Introduction), if it's just so you can be free from this sin that hounds you and have your friends and family respect you again, if it's so you can save your marriage or keep your job, then you have a wrong motive and God is not in the battle. You will not win (see Jas. 4:3).

So, the next time you feel overwhelmed in the fight, the next time you think God isn't helping you against this beast in your life, remember today's verse—remember what your sole duty is in this war and just do it.

"Fear the Lord your God, you and your son and your son's son, by keeping all his statutes and his commandments ... all the days of your life, and that your days may be long" (Deut. 6:2 ESV).

Additional reading: Ecclesiastes 8:12; Psalm 111:10; 112:1; 145:19; 147:11; Proverbs 19:23; 23:17.

Review, Assess, and Pray:
In the space below, answer the questions. Then, invest five minutes in prayer. Tell God your fears and struggles. Ask Him to open your heart and give you His strength to apply His truth to your life.

1) What did I learn from this?

2) What does God want me to do about it?

WEDNESDAY – NO POWER? PLUG IN!
Prayer Time:
It's the middle of the week—hump day. How are you doing? Are you staying consistent? If you're struggling with keeping to a daily routine with this, be sure to talk with your accountability partner. Ask him to pray with you about this.

Take a moment before you begin today and ask God to reveal Himself to you, to soften your heart to receive what He wants to tell you, and to give you the strength to apply it to your life.

Father, fill me with the knowledge of Your will in all spiritual wisdom and understanding so that I will walk today in a manner worthy of You, pleasing You in all respects, bearing fruit for You in everything I do, and increasing in my knowledge of You (Col. 1:10).

"His divine power has granted to us all things that pertain to life and godliness, through the knowledge of him who called us to his own glory and excellence." 2 Peter 1:3 (ESV)

Here's a question for you: Do you get mad at yourself for repeating the same sin over and over again? Have you ever said to yourself, "I can't believe I just did that"? Do you realize that is a form of pride? What we are really saying is, "I can't believe that a wonderful person like me would do such a thing!"

Think about it. Do you really believe that YOU can deal with this sin on your own? Read Philippians 4:13. It is only through Christ that we can win this war. Only God possesses the divine power to provide you with everything you need to be victorious and live a life that consistently glorifies Him. When you and I try to fight this on our own, we are denying the amazing power God has provided and claiming that ours is greater. Is it any wonder that we mess up?

Job asked the question, "Who can bring what is pure from the impure?" He then answers, "No one!" (Job 14:4; cp. Eccl. 7:20). In and of ourselves, we are incapable of living sexually pure lives. The only way we can be (and stay) on the victory side is when God Himself, who has that power, lives His life through us. And that happens when we consistently yield ourselves completely to Him (Rom. 6:12-14). This is why David declared that the only way to keep your heart pure was to live your life in complete obedience to God's Word (Psa. 119:9).

Peter assures us in our verse for today that God's divine power has already given you everything you need to be a sexually pure, godly man. Did you catch that? You already have exactly what you need to win the battle! You don't have to manufacture it or go searching for it. It's already within you in the person of the Holy Spirit.

Don't lose sight of the fact that this power to be godly comes as we grow in our knowledge of the Lord—as we focus our mind on Him (Col. 3:2). When the focus is off of self and on God, our actions will no longer be about self but about God. We are to always "be on (our) guard so that (we) are not carried away by the error of unprincipled men … but grow in the grace and knowledge of our Lord and Savior Jesus Christ" (2 Pet. 3:18 NASB).

The way out of the impurity trap is to know God deeply and personally. There is no other path to true change. Oh, don't get me wrong, other changes we do on our own might make life a little easier for the moment, but we are still ensnared in the same dark kingdom where self is sitting high on the throne.

Your goal: Know God in such a way that you will find Him far greater and more important to you than whatever else you love.

Review, Assess, and Pray:
In the space below, answer the questions. Then, invest five minutes in prayer. Tell God your fears and struggles. Ask Him to open your heart and give you His strength to apply His truth to your life.

1) What did I learn from this?

2) What does God want me to do about it?

THURSDAY – BUILDING ON THE ROCK
Prayer Time:
So how has your week been? What stresses are you facing that are attempting to pull you away from this devotional? Be sure to talk with your accountability partner about it. Ask him what stresses he is facing and pray together and for each other.

Take a moment before you begin today and ask God to reveal Himself to you, to soften your heart to receive what He wants to tell you, and to give you the strength to apply it to your life.

Father, I need you. Please fill me with the knowledge of Your will in all spiritual wisdom and understanding so that I will walk today in a manner worthy of You, pleasing You in all respects, bearing fruit for You in everything I do, and increasing in my knowledge of You (Col. 1:10).

"Everyone then who hears these words of mine and does them will be like a wise man who built his house on the rock. And the rain fell, and the floods came, and the winds blew and beat on that house, but it did not fall, because it had been founded on the rock. And everyone who hears these words of mine and does not do them will be like a foolish man who built his house on the sand. And the rain fell, and the floods came, and the winds blew and beat against that house, and it fell, and great was the fall of it." Matthew 7:24-27 (ESV)

If I asked you to describe your house, you probably would tell me such things as its location, color, design, square footage, possibly the size of the lot it sits on, and probably even the number of bedrooms and bathrooms. However, most likely you wouldn't tell me about the foundation. Yet, it is the foundation of your house that makes all the difference.

When building a home, it's rather important to start with a foundation. That only makes sense, right? After all, if you don't have a foundation, or if you build upon a weak one, it may stand for a brief period of time, but as soon as a strong wind comes along…WHAM! Down it goes.

Just as we need a solid foundation in order to build a solid structure, so we need to build a sexually pure life on a spiritually solid foundation. The bottom line is simple, if you expect to stay standing in the midst of the storms of sexual temptation that constantly hit you on every front, you need to be planted firmly on a foundation that will not fail—one that runs deep into solid rock.

In 1 Corinthians 3:11 we read, "For no one can lay a foundation other than that which is laid, which is Jesus Christ" (ESV). Think about that for a moment. There is only one foundation that we are to be building our lives upon. There is only one foundation that is guaranteed to keep us safe in the midst of the worst of storms. There is only one foundation that will hold you up while you are getting slammed with temptation. That foundation is none other than a growing and on-going relationship with Jesus Christ. If that's not what you're building on, your construction is happening on shifting sand and that is why you fail.

God alone is the Rock of our salvation (2 Sam. 22:47). As that Rock, He is our fortress, deliverer, shield, and stronghold in whom we take refuge (Psa. 18:1-2; 94:22). As we live our life on that Rock, He makes each step we take secure (Psa. 40:2).

A life that is built upon that Rock will never be greatly shaken (Psa. 62:2). And—praise God!—that Rock is immovable and everlasting (Isa. 26:4; cp. Heb. 13:8). That means we never, ever have to worry about it crumbling beneath us.

In our text for today, Jesus makes it clear that we *will* face storms that will try to shake us up and take us down. No matter how victorious you may be over sexual impurity, you will always encounter strong temptations.

Only when we are building our life into The Rock will we be able to weather the storm!

Review, Assess, and Pray:
In the space below, answer the questions. Then, invest five minutes in prayer. Tell God your fears and struggles. Ask Him to open your heart and give you His strength to apply His truth to your life.

1) What did I learn from this?

2) What does God want me to do about it?

FRIDAY – ARE YOU A WISE MAN?

Prayer Time:
As you head into your weekend, take a moment before you begin today and ask God to reveal Himself to you, to soften your heart to receive what He wants to tell you, and to give you the strength to apply it to your life.

Father, as I read this devotional, and as I meditate on Your Word throughout the day, fill me with the knowledge of Your will in all spiritual wisdom and understanding so that I will walk today in a manner worthy of You, pleasing You in all respects, bearing fruit for You in everything I do, and increasing in my knowledge of You (Col. 1:10).

"Everyone then who hears these words of mine and does them will be like a wise man who built his house on the rock. And the rain fell, and the floods came, and the winds blew and beat on that house, but it did not fall, because it had been founded on the rock. And everyone who hears these words of mine and does not do them will be like a foolish man who built his house on the sand. And the rain fell, and the floods came, and the winds blew and beat against that house, and it fell, and great was the fall of it." Matthew 7:24-27 (ESV)

Yesterday we talked about the Rock we must be building our life upon. Only then will we know safety and victory in the midst of the storms of temptation.

Today, let's take a few moments to notice the comparisons between the two builders in our text. First, they both shared a dream. They both had the same goal: build a house—build a good life worth living, a life that is significant and will leave a lasting legacy. What a vision!

No matter where you are in life, you are building as well. Whether you're just beginning or have been at it for years, every moment of every day—through every thought, every word, and every action—you are building your life. The question is: Of what quality are the materials you're using (1 Cor. 3:12-15)?

Now, let's consider the second comparison between these two builders. They were building their homes in the same neighborhood. They probably lived next door to each other. You see, they were both affected by the exact same storm at the same time. Jesus describes the storm precisely the same for both builders. The rain fell, the floods came, and the winds blew and beat against their house.

Again, no matter where you are in your building project, you too are going to face storms in life. Every one of us is affected by the same storms. We get rained on. We encounter those small, pesky, annoying drops of temptation that can quickly add up and drench us.

We get flooded. When we don't deal with our sins, they begin to back up and build up in our life. The damaging effects of those sins begin to erode away at the life we're trying to build. Just like flood waters, they sit there weighing heavy on us, leaving filthy gunk that clogs everything up and stops our ability to grow in Christ.

Finally, the winds slam into each of us. There are times when you will be blindsided by temptation. Sexual desire will blast you—seemingly out of nowhere—and push hard, trying to knock you down.

The fact is, life isn't always sunshine. It doesn't matter who you are or where you are spiritually, the storms of temptation will come. In fact, many times you'll get hit by rain *and* flooding *and* winds all at the same time. So don't be surprised when you face sexual temptation. Stand firm on the Rock. Though the storm may hit you full-force, and though it may feel like you can't bear up under it, because you've been building your life on Christ you will not fall!

Review, Assess, and Pray:
In the space below, answer the questions. Then, invest five minutes in prayer. Tell God your fears and struggles. Ask Him to open your heart and give you His strength to apply His truth to your life.

1) What did I learn from this?

2) What does God want me to do about it?

SATURDAY – JUST DO IT!

Prayer Time:

Breathe a sigh of relief—it's the weekend! Fight the temptation to take a break from your study. Stick to it, press on, and pause for a moment before you begin today, asking God to reveal Himself to you. Ask Him to soften your heart, enabling you to receive what He wants to tell you, and to give you the strength to apply it to your life.

Father, fill me with the knowledge of Your will in all spiritual wisdom and understanding so that I will walk today in a manner worthy of You, pleasing You in all respects, bearing fruit for You in everything I do, and increasing in my knowledge of You (Col. 1:10).

"Everyone then who hears these words of mine and does them will be like a wise man who built his house on the rock. And the rain fell, and the floods came, and the winds blew and beat on that house, but it did not fall, because it had been founded on the rock. And everyone who hears these words of mine and does not do them will be like a foolish man who built his house on the sand. And the rain fell, and the floods came, and the winds blew and beat against that house, and it fell, and great was the fall of it." Matthew 7:24-27 (ESV)

Today, let's consider the third comparison Jesus gives between the two builders. Both men went to the same Bible School. They sat in the same class and listened to the same Professor teach the same Bible lesson.

Jesus said they both "heard" His words. Both chose to be open to God's Truth. Please understand that Jesus wasn't saying the wise man had a love for hearing the truth, while the foolish man had utter contempt for it. No, both men heard God's Word. Both men sought it out. Both men knew the value of what God had to say. And both of these men *listened* to what the Lord said. Both of them gave careful consideration to what they heard, and they both understood how it applied to them!

Unfortunately, here is where the comparisons end. Here is where the men take two totally different paths. Here is where the single contrast makes one a wise man and the other foolish. Although they both were building their life, although they both faced the same storm, and although they both heard God's Word, the fundamental difference between the two was the foundation they chose to build upon. One chose obedience, the other did not.

Jesus said the wise man built his house upon the rock. He did this by immediately doing what God's Word instructed him to do. He let the truth of God's Word and the power of His principles infiltrate every fiber of his being to the point where they began flowing out of him in humble obedience.

The foolish man built his house upon the sand. He heard and understood what God wanted from him, yet he chose to ignore it. He felt he could handle life on his own. He was under the flesh-guided impression that God needed him instead of the other way around.

According to Luke 6:48, the wise man didn't simply set his house on that rock, he dug deep into it! Obedience requires effort; it calls for discipline. Remember, this wise man wasn't able to rent a 385 CAT Excavator, he didn't have access to a pneumatic jackhammer with alloy steel forgings and a four-bolt backhead design, he couldn't even find a simple stick of dynamite. He had just a chisel, a hammer, and sheer brute force.

It takes work to build on the Rock. It requires time and energy, and it costs more. Let's face it: it's always easier to take shortcuts in building a home. You save money when you use inferior materials. And for a while, no one may notice the shoddy work. But somewhere along the line, there is a price to be paid.

It also takes less time and energy to maintain a superficial faith. To be honest, who will be able to tell the difference? It's definitely easier to just show up for church for an hour a week, let the worship leader and the pastor fill you with warm-fuzzies, and then go on your way. It's less demanding on your day to just open the daily devotional booklet, read the few verses that are there, read the writer's comments, close it up, and go on with your day.

The question for you is: Are you *doing* the Word? Are you moment by moment, day by day choosing to do what God says? If you construct your life according to Christ's building codes, and if you dig deep into solid rock, you will not be disappointed (1 Pet. 2:6-7).

Review, Assess, and Pray:
In the space below, answer the questions. Then, invest five minutes in prayer. Tell God your fears and struggles. Ask Him to open your heart and give you His strength to apply His truth to your life.

1) What did I learn from this?

2) What does God want me to do about it?

AUTHENTIC ACCOUNTABILITY

This is an important time to share with your accountability partner. Discuss these questions in detail together. Challenge each other, be honest with each other, pray for each other, and don't be afraid to get into each other's lives. Be intentional, be real, and be ready for a blessing.

1. What did you learn from this week's set of devotions?

2. What changes need to take place in your life because of this?

3. What steps of faith are you going to take to make those changes?

4. Select at least one verse from this week to memorize. Explain why you chose that verse and how it applies to you.

WEEK THREE
Walking in the Word

Last week we talked about trying to fight this battle for purity on our own and why we will always fail when we do. We can't, but God can!

This week our devotions will take us on a journey through Psalm 19. Here we will discover the singular weapon God has provided us with that is guaranteed to take down the beast of sexual impurity in your life: The Word of God!

As I mentioned in the Introduction to this book, for over 30 years of my life I feebly attempted to gain victory over lust, porn, and masturbation, along with all the other selfish sexual satisfactions I was trying to pursue. No matter what I did, I failed. Then a man named Roger came alongside me and began to take me into the Bible.

Week after week we would open Scripture, study it, talk about it, and learn from it. I would be assigned a text to study during the week and a verse to memorize. Then I was required to return the following week and explain to Roger how it applied to my life and what I was going to do about it.

At first it was hard work! I was undisciplined and so my mind would wander. I would put off my assignment until the last possible moment. Roger would never accept my weak excuses for failure, and he would hold me accountable for my decisions. Slowly, change began to happen. I began to look forward to my time in the Word. I began to see God in a totally different light. I began to understand why I was making the sinful choices I had made and doing the sinful things I had done. Real change was happening in my heart!

Please understand that it wasn't because of Roger, it wasn't due to a particular counseling method, it wasn't even the result of my specific homework assignments that brought about change—it was because the Holy Spirit was implanting God's Truth into my heart and mind. God's Word is living, powerful, and active in our lives, sharper than any two-edged sword (Heb. 4:12). As we read it and study it, the words of our Creator and Heavenly Father begin to push aside all the junk in our life and address the real issues of our mind and heart.

So, as you dive into this week's devotions, consider the power of God's Word to provide us with everything we need to live a righteous, godly, and pure life (2 Pet. 1:3).

SUNDAY – OH, MERCY ME

Prayer Time:
Make sure you begin today by asking God to reveal Himself to you through this devotional and through the preaching of His Word. Ask Him to soften your heart so that you will receive what He wants to tell you. Let Him know you need Him to give you the strength to apply it to your life.

Father, fill me with the knowledge of Your will in all spiritual wisdom and understanding so that I will walk today in a manner worthy of You, pleasing You in all respects, bearing fruit for You in everything I do, and increasing in my knowledge of You (Col. 1:10).

"I urge you, brothers, in view of God's mercy, to offer your bodies as living sacrifices, holy and pleasing to God—this is your spiritual act of worship." Romans 12:1

Today, I trust you will join other believers in corporate worship of God. As you sing, as Scripture is read, and as the preacher delivers the sermon, I want to challenge you to think about God's amazingly wonderful and unconditional mercy.

"Mercy" is a word that refers to God's compassion and pity upon us. It has been said that His mercy is, "God not giving to us what we deserve." Think about that as you consider the sinful choices you made last week. Mull over for a moment how many times you put

44

self on the throne.   Now, reflect on what you *deserve* from a holy, righteous, and just God.

"He saved us, not because of works done by us in righteousness, but according to his own mercy, by the washing of regeneration and renewal of the Holy Spirit" (Tit. 3:5 ESV).   Peter said, "In (God's) great mercy He has given us new birth into a living hope through the resurrection of Jesus Christ from the Dead" (1 Pet. 1:3).   We deserve death, not life (Rom. 3:23).   Yet God, in His mercy, has declared that anyone who believes on His Son will not receive the death they deserve, but will have eternal life (1 Tim. 1:16)!

God's mercy is great (2 Sam. 24:14; 1 Chron. 21:13), and He shows us His great mercy because of His great love (Neh. 13:22; Psa. 25:6; Eph. 2:4).   It is because of God's mercy that He does not abandon us (Neh. 9:31), and that we are able to come boldly into His presence without fear (Psa. 5:7; Heb. 4:16).   God has promised His mercy to those who reject sinful thinking (putting self on the throne), turn to Him, and confess and renounce their sin (Prov. 28:13; Isa. 55:7).   In fact, God absolutely delights in showing us His mercy (Mic. 7:18).

So, *"in view of God's mercy"*—because of the fact that God has not given to us what we deserve—Paul urges us to offer our body to God. His call here is for believers to dedicate every aspect of themselves, without reservation, to the Lord.   Not just today, not just while in a Sunday worship service, but every moment of every day.

Notice also in our verse for today the word "offer."   In view of God's mercy, we are to *offer* our body to Him daily.   It's a technical term used to describe the way a priest places an offering on the altar with the intention of surrendering or yielding it up to God.   Anytime something was placed on an altar, it was for the purpose of sacrifice— willingly putting it to death, giving up ownership.

As a Christian, "you yourselves like living stones are being built up as a spiritual house, to be *a holy priesthood, to offer spiritual sacrifices* acceptable to God through Jesus Christ" (1 Pet. 2:5 ESV, emphasis mine). God considers you a "priest," and, as such, you are to offer—to daily surrender and yield—your body to Him. This is your priestly act of worship.

So this week, when you are tempted to give in to lust and the pull of sexual impurity, remember God's mercy and make your body available for God to employ for His glory instead of for you to use for sexual pleasure.

Review, Assess, and Pray:

In the space below, answer the questions. Then, invest five minutes in prayer. Tell God your fears and struggles. Ask Him to open your heart and give you His strength to apply His truth to your life.

    1) What did I learn from this?

    2) What does God want me to do about it?

MONDAY – DO YOU RESPECT THE LAW?

Prayer Time:

Take a moment before you begin today and ask God to reveal Himself to you, to soften your heart to receive what He wants to tell you, and to give you the strength to apply it to your life.

Father, I am asking right now that You fill me with the knowledge of Your will in all spiritual wisdom and understanding so that I will walk today in a manner worthy of You, pleasing You in all respects, bearing fruit for You in everything I do, and increasing in my knowledge of You (Col. 1:10).

"The law of the LORD is perfect, reviving the soul ..." **Psalm 19:7a**

Something has drastically shifted in Christianity. Collectively, as a body of believers, we have lost a respect for the law—God's law. I don't mean that we are blatantly throwing it out the window, thus doing whatever we want, and then acting like we don't care what

God thinks (although in some Christian circles that is happening). I'm referring to a smorgasbord mentality when it comes to Scripture.

We treat the Bible like a buffet table, reading God's Word, and then picking and choosing which laws and standards we like. We then opt to obey and follow them, leaving the rest to the "irrelevancy of Old Testament times." In our verse for today, King David tells us that God's law—*all* of God's law—is perfect. It was perfect then, and it is still perfect today.

Is that how you view the Bible? Can you say as David, "The law of (God's) mouth is better to me than thousands of gold and silver pieces" (Psa. 119:72 ESV)? Another way to put that verse is like this: God's Word is better to me than all the pornographic images in the world, and all the lustful thoughts and fantasies I could ever think or dream!

Can you honestly cry out, "Oh how I love your law! It is my meditation all the day" (Psa. 119:97 ESV)? Do you "love (God's) commandments above gold, above fine gold" (above sexual impurity), and do you "consider all (God's) precepts to be right" (Psa. 119:127-128 ESV)? In other words, does God really know what's best for you? Can you trust Him?

If you want genuine and lasting victory over sexual impurity, open your Bible daily! "Read in it all the days of (your) life ... learn to fear the Lord (your) God by keeping all the words of (God's) law and these statutes, and (do) them" (Deut. 17:19 ESV)! Don't let "this Book of the Law ... depart from your mouth, but ... meditate on it day and night, so that you may be careful to do according to all that is written in it. For then you will make your way prosperous"—and then you will know victory over lust and sexual impurity in your life (Josh. 1:8 ESV)!

Look again at our verse for today. God's Word is perfect! It is complete, whole, and entire, lacking in nothing. In other words, it has the answer for every problem, it gives the weapons you need for every battle, and it will help you slay the dragon. "(Our) God— his way is perfect; the word of the Lord proves true; he is a shield for all those who take refuge in him" (Psa. 18:30 ESV).

So this week—every day—make the time to dig into God's Word. It will revive you. It will refresh and restore you. It will help you to say "No" to lust and sexual impurity, and return to the God who loves you.

> My soul clings to the dust; give me life according to your word! When I told of my ways, you answered me; teach me your statutes! Make me understand the way of your precepts, and I will meditate on your wondrous works. My soul melts away for sorrow; strengthen me according to your word! Put false ways far from me and graciously teach me your law! I have chosen the way of faithfulness; I set your rules before me. I cling to your testimonies, O Lord; let me not be put to shame! I will run in the way of your commandments when you enlarge my heart! (Psa. 119:25-32 ESV)

Review, Assess, and Pray:
In the space below, answer the questions. Then, invest five minutes in prayer. Tell God your fears and struggles. Ask Him to open your heart and give you His strength to apply His truth to your life.

1) What did I learn from this?

2) What does God want me to do about it?

TUESDAY – WISE UP WISE GUY
Prayer Time:
I commend you for plugging away at this every day. God has a plan for your life so take a moment before you begin today and ask Him to show Himself to you in a very real way. Look for Him to soften your heart so you can receive what He wants to tell you, and to give you the strength to apply it to your life.

Father, fill me with the knowledge of Your will in all spiritual wisdom and understanding so that I will walk today in a manner worthy of You, pleasing You in all respects, bearing fruit for You in everything I do, and increasing in my knowledge of You (Col. 1:10).

"...The testimony of the LORD is sure, making wise the simple."
Psalm 19:7b (ESV)

Typically a "testimony" is considered to be a statement given to tell others about a specific event or experience they had. We often give our testimony in church, sharing how we came to know Christ as our Savior and all that He has done in our life.

Here, the "testimony of the LORD" simply refers to what God has to say about Himself. It is a phrase David uses to speak of Scripture, for that is where we learn about God. So in essence, David is saying that God's Word is sure—it's reliable and trustworthy. When God says something, you can take it to the bank. You see, "All his precepts are trustworthy, they are established forever and ever, to be performed with faithfulness and uprightness" (Psa. 111:7-8 ESV).

Take a close, hard look at your life. Can you honestly say that God's "testimonies are (your) delight; they are (your) counselors" (Psa. 119:24 ESV)? Do you delight in God's Word "as much as in all riches" (Psa. 119:14 ESV)? Is the Bible your "heritage forever ... the joy of (your) heart" (Psa. 119:111 ESV)? It should be. Why? Only through Scripture are we able to grow in Christ and be victorious over lust.

To win our battle against sexual impurity, we must grasp the vital necessity of growing in our relationship with God. To grow in Christ you must daily:

Give Him your heart and mind (Prov. 23:26; cp. Prov. 4:23; 23:19; 28:26; Matt. 22:37)
Read the Bible (Rom. 15:4; cp. Prov. 4:13; Psa. 32:8; Matt. 4:4; 2 Tim. 3:16-17)
Obey what God reveals to you (Jn. 14:15, 23; cp. 1 Jn. 2:4-5; 5:3)
Work out your faith (Phil. 2:12; cp. Gal. 6:7-9; Heb. 12:1; 1 Pet. 2:12; Phil. 1:27)

Our verse for today says that God's Word is not only trustworthy, but it will make you wise. Wisdom has been defined as the skillful use of knowledge. In other words, when you read God's Word, you gain knowledge—you learn who God is and what He expects of you. When you invest your time every day in the study and memorization of Scripture, and then throughout the day meditate on what the Holy Spirit is revealing to you, God promises that you will become wise. You will understand how to apply what you have learned to your own life. You will begin to actually live a life that glorifies God.

"The unfolding of (God's) words gives light; it imparts understanding to the simple" (Psa. 119:130 ESV). When you memorize Scripture, and when you hide God's Word in your heart, it becomes a great deterrent to sin (Psa. 119:9, 11). Why? It is God's Word that "makes (you) wiser than (your) enemies, for it is ever with (you)." As you dig into Scripture, you will "have more understanding than all (your) teachers, for (God's) testimonies are (your) meditation" (Psa. 119:98-100).

I cannot overemphasize the importance and the necessity of investing your time daily to be in the Word. If you want to know how to defeat the dragon of sexual impurity, and if you want to live a life that honors and glorifies God, you must fill your mind with the testimony of the Lord that is trustworthy. As you apply the truth to your life, as you walk in obedience to God's standards, you will be wise—you will be free!

Review, Assess, and Pray:
In the space below, answer the questions. Then, invest five minutes in prayer. Tell God your fears and struggles. Ask Him to open your heart and give you His strength to apply His truth to your life.

1) What did I learn from this?

2) What does God want me to do about it?

WEDNESDAY – FOLLOW THE INSTRUCTIONS
Prayer Time:
We don't know what God has in store for you today, so take a moment before you begin this devotional and ask God to reveal Himself to you, to soften your heart to receive what He wants to tell you, and to give you the strength to apply it to your life.

Father, fill me with the knowledge of Your will in all spiritual wisdom and understanding so that I will walk today in a manner worthy of You, pleasing You in all respects, bearing fruit for You in everything I do, and increasing in my knowledge of You (Col. 1:10).

"The precepts of the LORD are right, rejoicing the heart …" Psalm 19:8a (ESV)

God has a code of conduct for His children, a certain behavior He expects from each of us. David called them "precepts." Precepts are the Scriptural guidelines that provide us the principles of life.

A great example of a precept from God is found in 1 Corinthians 10:31, which says, "Whether you eat or drink, or whatever you do, do all to the glory of God" (ESV). Another one is this: "Whatever you do, in word or deed, do everything in the name of the Lord Jesus, giving thanks to God the Father through him" (Col. 3:17 ESV). Here is another one to consider: "Among you there must not be even a hint of sexual immorality" (Eph. 5:3).

Do you understand why God gave us His precepts? God's code of conduct gives us the tools we need to maintain a close relationship with Him. They are God's boundaries that give us an amazing freedom in serving Him. Please, my friend, don't look at Scripture as a set of rules handed to you by a God who is distant, detached, and doesn't care about you. Don't look at God as someone who is sitting up in Heaven just waiting for you to screw up so He can zap you.

God isn't out to make your life miserable, He has amazing plans for you, plans to bless you beyond your wildest imaginations (Jer. 29:11). I know that when you are in the thick of the battle against impurity it sure doesn't seem that way. That is the time we must desperately cling to God's promises and trust Him completely. That is the time we must fight to be in God's Word!

To know God's blessing and to experience victory over sexual impurity in your life, God has given you a set of guidelines. These precepts are trustworthy—in other words, they actually work! (Psa. 111:7). They show you how to live in a way that is not only free from impurity, but will glorify Him. He wants you to keep these precepts diligently (Psa. 119:4). Why? Follow them and you will be free. Don't lose sight of our verse for today—God's precepts are right, they will never lead you wrong (Psa. 119:128)!

We should strive to be like King David who deeply desired to know God's code of conduct (Psa. 119:40). In fact, he loved God's precepts (Psa. 119:159) and meditated on them, always fixing his eyes on God's ways (Psa. 119:15). This is why he was described as a man after God's own heart (Acts 13:22). He kept company only with others who were seeking God's precepts as well (Psa. 119:63). What are your eyes fixed on? With whom do you associate and keep company? Who do you spend your time with?

When we seek out God's precepts and walk in them, we are walking in a wide place (Psa. 119:45). We will know God's richest blessings on our life (Psa. 119:56). Oh, that doesn't mean we will be free from temptation, and it doesn't mean we won't have to fight the battle anymore (Psa. 119:87, 110). It does mean that He is there as our refuge, our fortress, and our solid rock who will save us from destruction (Psa. 119:94).

Listen one more time today to David as he talks about God's wonderful precepts:

- "Through your precepts I get understanding; therefore I hate every false way." Psa. 119:104 (ESV)
- "I consider all your precepts to be right; I hate every false way." Psa. 119:128 (ESV)

Review, Assess, and Pray:
In the space below, answer the questions. Then, invest five minutes in prayer. Tell God your fears and struggles. Ask Him to open your heart and give you His strength to apply His truth to your life.

1) What did I learn from this?

2) What does God want me to do about it?

THURSDAY – OBEDIENCE IS THE VERY BEST WAY

Prayer Time:
Before you begin today, thank God for what He's been teaching you and ask Him to reveal Himself to you through today's study. Ask Him to continue to soften your heart so you can receive what He wants to tell you, and then to give you the strength to apply it to your life.

Father, fill me with the knowledge of Your will in all spiritual wisdom and understanding so that I will walk today in a manner worthy of You, pleasing You in all respects, bearing fruit for You in everything I do, and increasing in my knowledge of You (Col. 1:10).

"... The commandment of the LORD is pure, enlightening the eyes."
Psalm 19:8b (ESV)

When you read the word "commandment," what comes to mind? Let's consider it in military terms. "Command" is the authority a person in the military lawfully exercises over subordinates by virtue of his rank and position. The purpose of that command is to influence others to accomplish the mission by providing purpose, direction, and motivation.

Although the subordinate may not understand or agree with the command, he is to follow his orders to the letter, trusting that his commander not only sees a bigger picture (the ultimate mission) but also has a plan and a purpose.

God is our Commander-in-Chief and we will stand before Him someday to answer for our actions—did we follow His orders or not (2 Cor. 5:10; cp. 1 Sam 2:3; Psa. 50:6; Eccl. 12:14; Rom. 14:11-12)?

The word David uses for "commandment" here literally means "words of wisdom." God is not blindly moving pawns around on a chessboard just to get His jollies. He has a plan and a purpose for your life—a mission for you, if you will. In great wisdom He instructs you in the task He has called you to. Job asked the question, "Where shall wisdom be found? And where is the place of understanding" (Job 28:12 ESV)? The answer is, "With God are wisdom and might; *he* has counsel and understanding" (Job 12:13 ESV, emphasis added). You see, God's "wisdom is profound, His power is vast" (Job 9:4). We can trust that He knows what He's doing!

In earlier years, before technology enhanced the ability of armies to communicate with each other, a courier would be dispatched with written orders. Once received, the written command was to be completed. If the orders were not followed, if the senior officer on the field disregarded the command in favor of his own plan, he might win the skirmish but the battle could be in jeopardy.

In a sense, that's what our Bible is: written orders from our Commander-in-Chief, God Himself. These commands are not to be taken lightly; they are to be followed. They're not up for our own personal interpretation, they are words of wisdom from the One who sees the whole battlefield and understands the movements of the enemy.

In our battle against sexual impurity, our Commander has given us marching orders. He has told us how to fight (Jas. 4:7), how to stand (1 Cor. 16:13; Gal. 5:1; Eph. 6:13), and what weapon to use (Eph. 6:17). Ours is not to question His command or doubt His wisdom. Ours is not to try to figure out how on earth that method or weapon is going to work when everything else we tried failed. The responsibility that falls upon us as soldiers is to obey.

Look again at our verse for today. God's commands are pure. They are clean, without error, without deceit, and without an ulterior motive. Follow them and one day you will see the bigger picture as your spiritual eyes begin to see what He is doing in your life.

I can remember a song my kids used to sing in Sunday school. It said, *"Obedience is the very best way to show that you believe. Doing exactly what the Lord commands, doing it happily. Action is the key, do it immediately, joy you will receive. Obedience is the very best way to show that you believe!"*

Review, Assess, and Pray:
In the space below, answer the questions. Then, invest five minutes in prayer. Tell God your fears and struggles. Ask Him to open your heart and give you His strength to apply His truth to your life.

1) What did I learn from this?

2) What does God want me to do about it?

FRIDAY – DO YOU SEE WHAT I SEE?

Prayer Time:
As you approach the weekend, take a moment before you begin today's devotional and ask God to reveal Himself to you, to soften your heart to receive what He wants to tell you, and to give you the strength to apply it to your life.

Father, fill me with the knowledge of Your will in all spiritual wisdom and understanding so that I will walk today in a manner worthy of You, pleasing You in all respects, bearing fruit for You in everything I do, and increasing in my knowledge of You (Col. 1:10).

"... The commandment of the LORD is pure, enlightening the eyes." Psalm 19:8b (ESV)

Yesterday we looked at the first part of this verse, talking about the necessity of trusting in and following the Lord's commands. Today let's zero in on the last part of the verse, namely that God's Word is so pure it enlightens the eyes.

Do you want to know how to effectively say "No!" to sexual temptation? Do you desire to stop giving in to lust and the pull of porn? Do you long for the time when you never have to lie to cover up your sin? God can show you how! Solomon said, "The LORD gives wisdom; from his mouth come knowledge and understanding" (Prov. 2:6 ESV).

It begins by daily opening your Bible and letting the truth and wisdom of God's Word penetrate your heart and mind (Heb. 4:12). As it does, your eyes will be opened and you will see what you need to do, where you need to go, and how to accomplish it. One of the primary ministries of the Holy Spirit in your life is to guide you into all of God's Truth (Jn. 16:13; 1 Cor. 2:10-13). Open your Bible my friend, and let Him do that.

God promises that through His Word "(He guides) you in the way of wisdom and (leads) you along straight paths" (Prov. 4:11). David declares in our verse for today that God's words of wisdom are radiant (pure); they enlighten our eyes. In other words, God's wisdom gives light to help you see the way to victory; it illuminates your path.

Think about this: those words of wisdom are found in Scripture. So every time you invest time opening your Bible and studying God's Word, the verses you read act as "a lamp to (your) feet and a light for (your) path" (Psa. 119:105). They are a massive spotlight pouring pure white light on your life saying, "This is the way to victory, walk in it!"

Recently I was sitting at my computer when a nasty mosquito landed on my brow and began to feast. I quickly slapped my hand to my forehead and nailed the little bugger. Pulling my hand away I saw not only the smudge of the bug, but blood. So, with a sigh, I went into the bathroom to deal with it. Wouldn't you know, when I looked in the mirror I couldn't see anything. I had to turn the light on. The brightness of the light allowed me to see the problem and deal with it.

When my mind is focused on self—when the goal of my life is to please King Me—every decision I make, every word I speak, every thing I do will be focused on that singular goal: self-satisfaction. I'm working in the dark and so I can't see what needs to be done to deal with my sin issues. It will seem like I'm making good decisions at the time, but that way is always the wrong way (Prov. 14:12; 16:25; 30:12; cp. Jas. 1:22).

The only way to know where God wants you to be and what God wants you to do is to dig into Scripture daily. "The words of the Lord are pure words, like silver refined in a furnace on the ground, purified seven times" (Psa. 12:6 ESV). "Every word of God proves true" (Prov. 30:5 ESV). This means that "the unfolding of (God's) words gives light; it imparts understanding to the simple" (Psa. 119:130 ESV).

Review, Assess, and Pray:
In the space below, answer the questions. Then, invest five minutes in prayer. Tell God your fears and struggles. Ask Him to open your heart and give you His strength to apply His truth to your life.

1) What did I learn from this?

2) What does God want me to do about it?

SATURDAY – ARE DESIRES BAD?

Prayer Time:
Saturdays can be busy days as we try to get projects done, or make some time to relax after a hard week. Your dedication to this devotional is not going unnoticed. Take a moment right now and ask God to reveal Himself to you, to soften your heart to receive what He wants to tell you, and to give you the strength to apply it to your life.

Father, fill me with the knowledge of Your will in all spiritual wisdom and understanding so that I will walk today in a manner worthy of You, pleasing You in all respects, bearing fruit for You in everything I do, and increasing in my knowledge of You (Col. 1:10).

———————————

"More to be desired are they than gold, even much fine gold; sweeter also than honey and drippings of the honeycomb. Moreover, by them is your servant warned; in keeping them there is great reward." Psalm 19:10-11 (ESV)

One of the greatest struggles we face in the war against sexual impurity in our lives is on the battlefield of misplaced desires. The lie of Satan is that "I *need* this" and "I *deserve* that." We get caught up in believing that our sinful sexual desires are somehow justified because our particular situation is "unique." We are convinced that "feeling good" will help us cope.

Look carefully at our verse for today. We learned this week that the Scriptures are perfect, sure, right, pure, clean, and true. When you saturate your mind and fill your heart with God's Word it revives your soul, makes you wise, rejoices your heart, and enlightens your eyes. Why on earth would we desire anything more than we desire a close walk with God through our study of His Word?

Unfortunately, the answer to that question is all too true for the majority of us. You see, we have learned to focus our thoughts and feelings on pleasing self instead of pleasing God. We are on a quest to find personal satisfaction instead of being on a mission to honor our Creator, Savior, and Friend. As a result, we don't see God (or His Word) as someone (or something) that will "meet my needs" and "provide me with pleasure." This, in turn, creates in me a wrong desire. That desire leads me down a bad path where I make sinful choices.

In today's verse, David uses the word "desire" to refer to taking great pleasure in something—namely, God's Word. Do you take great pleasure in God's Word? Can you say as David did, "Oh how I *love* your law! It is my meditation all the day" (Psa. 119:97 ESV, emphasis added; cp. Psa. 119:127)? He began the book of Psalms by saying that the man who knows God's blessing on his life is the man whose "delight is in the law of the Lord, and on his law he meditates day and night" (Psa. 1:2 ESV).

More to be desired is God's law, God's truth, and God's standards of righteousness and holiness than any lustful thought or sexual fantasy. I know that to many it sounds boring, dull, and mind-numbingly pointless. After all, how can I possibly find reading my Bible to be more pleasurable than lust, porn, fantasies, masturbation, and other sexual impurities?

The reason we battle with this, the reason we struggle with comprehending something that seems so incomprehensible, is because we don't really know God. We haven't invested the time yet in digging for the treasures He has buried for us in His Word. We are too focused on the here and now, on the tangible things we can touch, see, and feel in the moment.

This is one of the primary reasons for this devotional guide: to take you into Scripture daily and to get you to meditate on the Word of God, seeking the God of the Word. I assure you, as a man who spent 30 years of his life pursuing sexual pleasure, God's Word is truly sweeter—more pleasant—than any sexual fantasy or extra-marital affair.

God's Word is powerful (Heb. 4:12) if you but let it work in your heart. As our verse says, not only is it worth more than gold and sweet to the taste, but also by it we are warned. As we walk in obedience to it, the end result is great gain—a deep relationship with the Almighty God who loves you more than you will ever know.

Review, Assess, and Pray:
In the space below, answer the questions. Then, invest five minutes in prayer. Tell God your fears and struggles. Ask Him to open your heart and give you His strength to apply His truth to your life.

1) What did I learn from this?

2) What does God want me to do about it?

AUTHENTIC ACCOUNTABILITY

Think about what we discovered this week. God's Word gives you instructions on how to live, rules and guidelines on the principles of life, a code of conduct to abide by, and words of wisdom that will show you the way to purity.

God's Word is complete, whole, entire, lacking in nothing, trustworthy, always right, it will never take you down the wrong path because it will always light the way. It enables you to stay morally and spiritually pure, it is firm, reliable, completely just and right, and it is the final authority in your life!

1. What did you learn about yourself from this week's set of devotions?

2. What did you learn about God from this week's set of devotions?

3. What changes need to take place in your life because of this?

4. What steps of faith are you taking to make those changes?

5. Select at least one verse from this week to memorize. Explain why you chose that verse and how it applies to you.

WEEK FOUR
Preventing a Spiritual Heart Attack

When you think about a massive heart attack, you probably imagine someone who suddenly clutches his chest and collapses. We know that a heart attack of any proportion is not something to play around with; seconds count in getting the proper treatment and saving a life.

A heart attack occurs because the circulation of blood to the heart muscle is blocked. If that blockage is not rapidly opened, heart tissue will die from a lack of oxygen, resulting in permanent heart damage and life-threatening problems.

I am told that the prevention of a heart attack is fairly straightforward. Don't smoke or use tobacco, exercise regularly, eat a heart-healthy diet, maintain a healthy weight, get enough quality sleep, and see your doctor for regular health screenings (resource - mayoclinic.org).

Spiritually speaking, we are all born with a serious heart condition. Jeremiah declared, "The heart is deceitful above all things, and desperately sick" (Jer. 17:9 ESV). When God looked at man's condition, "The Lord saw that the wickedness of man was great in the earth, and that every intention of the thoughts of his heart was only evil continually" (Gen 6:5 ESV).

Solomon, in all of his God-given wisdom acknowledged that "as (a man) thinketh in his heart, so is he" (Prov. 23:7 KJV). In other words, the condition of our heart determines the condition of our life. This is evidenced by the fact that "The fool says in his heart, 'There is no God'"—the condition of his heart. As a result, he is "corrupt, doing abominable iniquity"—the condition of his life (Psa. 53:1 ESV). You see, "Out of the heart come ... adultery (and) sexual immorality" (Matt. 15:19; Mark 7:21-22 ESV).

If you have come to a point in your life where you acknowledged your heart condition—your state of sinful rebellion against God (read Rom. 1:18-2:16; 3:23)—and you have confessed your sinfulness before God (1 Jn. 1:9), believing in your heart that Jesus (the Son of God) died on the cross of Calvary to pay the price for your sinful and rebellious heart (Jn. 3:16-18), then God Himself says you are saved (Acts 16:31; cp. Rom. 6:23; 10:9)!

At the moment of your salvation that old sinful heart was crucified—put to death (Gal. 2:20). Your hardened, calloused, and rebellious heart of stone was removed and God gave you a new heart (Ezek. 11:19; 36:26; cp. 2 Cor. 5:17). You've had a total heart transplant. Isn't that fantastic!

A friend of ours recently went through a heart transplant. Since having this new heart, she has had to change some aspects of her life. There are certain things she has to stay away from. She has to eat a proper diet, she must do certain exercises, she must take periods of rest, she must take certain medications, and she must see her doctor regularly.

In a similar way, once you have become a born-again believer—once you have been given that new heart—you must "above all else, guard your heart, for it is the wellspring of life" (Prov. 4:23).

This week we are going to see in God's Word how to maintain a healthy "heart" so we can live a "healthy" life that glorifies God in everything we think, say, and do.

SUNDAY – ARE YOU STAYING CLEAR OR DRAWING NEAR?

Prayer Time:
This is a day to focus our full attention on God. Don't neglect today's devotional. Make the time to work through this text. Be sure to take a moment before you begin and ask God to reveal Himself to you, to soften your heart to receive what He wants to tell you, and to give you the strength to apply it to your life.

Father, fill me with the knowledge of Your will in all spiritual wisdom and understanding so that I will walk today in a manner worthy of You, pleasing You in all respects, bearing fruit for You in everything I do, and increasing in my knowledge of You (Col. 1:10).

"This people draw near with their mouth and honor me with their lips, while their hearts are far from me, and their fear of me is a commandment taught by men."   Isaiah 29:13 (ESV)

Today, as you join others at church in corporate worship of God, ask yourself one very important question: I understand my body is here to worship, but is my heart?

Moses told Aaron to "draw near to the altar and offer your sin offering" (Lev. 9:7 ESV). James urges us to "draw near to God, and he will draw near to you. Cleanse your hands, you sinners, and purify your hearts, you double-minded" (Jas. 4:8 ESV). Is your heart pure as you draw near to God Almighty?

Today, as you worship, your purpose should be to draw near to God. The intention of church isn't for you to "go and get" something out of it, but to come boldly before God's throne to give of yourself and all you are to the One who gave it all for you. Can you say along with David, "For me, it is good to be near God"? (Psa. 73:28).

We are encouraged to "with confidence draw near to the throne of grace" (Heb. 4:16 ESV). In fact, we are given the promise that when we draw near to God, He will draw near to us (Jas. 4:8). This is what worship is all about—glorifying Him "in the splendor of holiness" (Psa. 29:2 ESV). That will happen only as we seek first His kingdom and righteousness in every aspect of our life (Matt. 6:33).

However, God also made it abundantly clear that "no one who has a blemish shall draw near" (Lev. 21:18 ESV). In other words, when I hold on to sin in my heart, drawing near to God means nothing—my praise and my worship is worthless (Psa. 66:18; cp. Prov. 28:9). I must first cleanse my hands and purify my heart (Jas. 4:8). Otherwise, just as our verse for today says, we are just people who pretend to draw near to God on the outside, while on the inside our hearts are far from Him.

If "the words of my mouth and the meditation of my heart" are going to "be acceptable in (God's) sight" (Psa. 19:14 ESV), then I must begin by crying out: "Create in me a clean heart, O God, and renew a right spirit within me" (Psa. 51:10 ESV)!

What is the condition of your heart today? Do you have unconfessed sin? Have you been sexually impure this past week with your mind? Have you done things that were even slightly improper sexually (Eph. 5:3)? Drawing near to God always requires us to "draw near with a true heart in full assurance of faith, with our hearts sprinkled clean" (Heb. 10:22 ESV; cp. 2 Tim. 2:21).

So again I ask, as you go to church today to worship, are you drawing near with your mouth and honoring Him with your lips (the things you say, the songs you sing, the smile on your face as you greet others), yet your heart is not right with God?

Consider this as you walk through the doors of your church: You must draw near to your Heavenly Father specifically to listen to what He wants to say to you rather than to offer Him your praise. "Guard your steps when you go to the house of God. To draw near to listen is better than to offer the sacrifice of fools" (Eccl. 5:1 ESV).

Don't be like the men described in Ezekiel, men who

> Come to (God), as they usually do, and sit before (God) to listen to (His) words, but they do not put them into practice. With their mouths they express devotion, but their hearts are greedy for unjust gain. Indeed, to them (God is) nothing more than one who sings love songs with a beautiful voice and plays an instrument well, for they hear (God's) words but do not put them into practice. (Ezek. 33:31-32)

Review, Assess, and Pray:
In the space below, answer the questions. Then, invest five minutes in prayer. Tell God your fears and struggles. Ask Him to open your heart and give you His strength to apply His truth to your life.

1) What did I learn from this?

2) What does God want me to do about it?

MONDAY - ABSTINENCE: THE WAY OF LIFE
Prayer Time:
As we begin week four, take a moment right now and ask God to reveal Himself to you in a mighty way. Ask Him to soften your heart so that you can receive what He wants to tell you. Then, ask Him to give you the strength to apply it to your life (Phil. 4:13).

Father, fill me with the knowledge of Your will in all spiritual wisdom and understanding so that I will walk today in a manner worthy of You, pleasing You in all respects, bearing fruit for You in everything I do, and increasing in my knowledge of You (Col. 1:10).

"Beloved, I urge you as sojourners and exiles to abstain from the passions of the flesh, which wage war against your soul." **1 Peter 2:11 (ESV)**

Our theme for this week is focused on preventing a spiritual heart attack. A person who has had a heart transplant is instructed by their doctor to stay away from certain things if they want their heart to be (and remain) healthy. For example, smoking raises blood pressure which increases the risk of stroke. The chemicals and compounds in a cigarette can harm your heart as well (source: texasheart.org). To ignore the doctor's warnings and partake anyway could mean serious damage to the heart and thus directly impact their life in a negative way.

As a born-again believer you have been given a heart transplant (Jer. 24:7; Ezek. 11:19; 36:26). Your Great Physician, God Himself, has given you a similar instruction—stay away from certain things if you want your spiritual heart to remain healthy. For example, "This is the will of God, your sanctification: that you abstain from sexual immorality" (1 Thess. 4:3 ESV). Could the Savior of your soul be any clearer? To protect your spiritual heart, totally abstain from what Peter called the "passions of the flesh, which wage war against your soul."

When we look at porn, when we lust in our heart, when we fantasize and masturbate, when we look with our eyes and linger, and when we allow our thoughts to dwell on sexual impurity we are injecting our new heart with a terrible poison. We are training our heart to focus on and yield to the sinful desires of the flesh instead of the godly desires of the Spirit.

To abstain from something means you are restraining yourself from indulging in that which—although giving the appearance of being good for you—can be harmful to your well-being. Think about that for a moment. To abstain from something requires effort. To abstain means you are forcibly holding yourself back from doing something your flesh wants. Paul describes it as an ongoing battle that made him miserable (Rom. 7:15-25). A battle we also fight—one to which we must never give in.

The reality is, your flesh will always crave pleasure. This is because your flesh is still governed by sin. Paul said, "I know that nothing good dwells in me, that is, in my flesh" (Rom. 7:18 ESV). In fact, with the flesh we will always give in to sin (Rom. 7:25). We will always yield to "sexual immorality, impurity, sensuality" (Gal. 5:19 ESV).

Jesus described the flesh as being weak (Matt. 26:41) and of no help at all (Jn. 6:63). When you live according to the flesh, your mind will be focused on what the flesh wants (Rom. 8:5). When your mind is set on getting what the flesh wants, you are going against God (Rom. 8:7) and nothing you do will please him (Rom. 8:8). You are damaging your new heart.

Take care of the new heart God has given you! Stay away my friend—far, far away from lust, pornography, self-gratification, and all the other areas and aspects of sexual impurity. Don't even let a hint of it into your life. The only way to ensure a healthy heart is to totally, unreservedly, and at all times abstain from sexual immorality, refusing to follow any form of the passions of the flesh.

Review, Assess, and Pray:
In the space below, answer the questions. Then, invest five minutes in prayer. Tell God your fears and struggles. Ask Him to open your heart and give you His strength to apply His truth to your life.

1) What did I learn from this?

2) What does God want me to do about it?

TUESDAY – EAT HEALTHY, EAT RIGHT
Prayer Time:
O my dear Father, please fill me with the knowledge of Your will as I read today's devotional. I ask You to give me spiritual wisdom and understanding so that I will walk this day—all day—in a manner worthy of You, pleasing You in all respects, bearing fruit for You in everything I do, and increasing in my knowledge of You (Col. 1:10).

_____

"Why do you spend your money for that which is not bread, and your labor for that which does not satisfy? Listen diligently to me, and eat what is good, and delight yourselves in rich food. Incline your ear, and come to me; hear, that your soul may live." Isaiah 55:2-3 (ESV)

In the fight against heart disease, a healthy diet and lifestyle are your best weapons. So although, for example, eating things high in sodium won't instantly kill you, it's probably not very wise to consume them in great quantities. Doctors tell us to eat more fish, limit our meat and dairy, count our cholesterol, fill up on fruits, vegetables, and whole grains, and go easy on the caffeine. Why? Because what we take into our body can directly impact the health of our heart.

In the same way, we need to watch what we "eat" spiritually. Look again at our verse for today. Why do you spend your time, energy, and all else that God has blessed you with on that which cannot truly feed you. Why waste it on that which does not satisfy you and meet your needs? Let's face it, porn, lust, and masturbation (and all other forms of sexual impurity) definitely fit into this category. We spend our time trying to satisfy self, only to come away empty, unfulfilled, and wanting more.

God is calling you to put all of your attention on Him. He knows what's best for your heart. He knows what will make you spiritually healthy and help you grow, and He's prepared a special meal just for you! We need to open our Bible every day for the rest of our lives and feed on every word that comes from God's mouth (Matt. 4:4).

Unlike most "heart healthy" foods that can leave a lot to be desired in the taste department, the food that God has prepared for you is "rich." Jeremiah said, "Your words were found, and I ate them, and your words became to me a joy and the delight of my heart, for I am called by your name, O LORD, God of hosts" (Jer. 15:16 ESV). As we feed daily upon Scripture, it delights our heart. In other words, it's good for you! The opposite is equally as true—if you do not feed daily upon God's Word, your heart will become weak and sick.

Are you eating healthy? Keep in mind that if you are not feeding on the Word of God, you are feeding on something. We need to starve the sinful flesh. Stop looking at porn. Stop letting your mind drift away on the waves of fantasy. We need to feed on the Word of God and let God be the strength of our heart and our portion forever (Psa. 73:26; cp. 2 Cor. 4:16).

I'm sure you probably can quote this next text, but please pause right now and take a moment to read Psalm 23. Our Shepherd makes sure we have the finest pastures to graze in. Did you know that sheep only lie down when they are full? God's Word fills us, it guides us, it restores us, it protects us, and it comforts us. Why on earth would you want to go anywhere else to eat when He has prepared the best table possible for you!

If you want victory in your life over the beast of sexual impurity, you must build up your strength by eating right—feeding upon Scripture daily. Being fed from the pulpit on Sunday is great, but it must never be enough. Being read to has its place, but we need to read Scripture ourselves if we're going to grow. The value of a meal isn't in being handed the menu.

You must take it even further though, if you want lasting change. You need to be like the saints in Berea that "examined the Scriptures every day" (Ac. 17:11). Study God's Word each and every day, my friend. Examine it. Dig into it. Make the time to search for the hidden treasures God has for you (Prov. 2:4; cp. Col. 2:3). Remember that the only difference between reading the Bible and studying it is a pen and paper. Yet what a difference that study can make.

Finally, memorize and meditate on what you've studied—then obey it. Now I can almost hear a collective groan rising in the throats of most of you reading this. Memorize? Seriously? Why memorize? The Holy Spirit's primary ministry today is to remind you of the things God has said to you (Jn. 14:26). Think about this: You cannot remember something you do not know. You tried it in High School and college right? It didn't work then, and it certainly won't work now, either. So buck up, be a man—memorize! Give the Holy Spirit the tools He needs to remind you of God's truth in the moment of temptation.

Why meditate? Meditating on Scripture, mulling it over in your mind, thinking about what God is saying and how it applies to you personally, will enable you to then walk in obedience. God promises that when you do, you will prosper and be successful (Josh. 1:8; Psa. 19:14; 119:97).

Finally, obey it. Never forget that God is "watching to see that (His) word is fulfilled" (Jer. 1:12).

Review, Assess, and Pray:
In the space below, answer the questions. Then, invest five minutes in prayer. Tell God your fears and struggles. Ask Him to open your heart and give you His strength to apply His truth to your life.

   1) What did I learn from this?

   2) What does God want me to do about it?

WEDNESDAY – EXERCISE DOES A HEART GOOD

Prayer Time:
Father, as I read today's devotional, please fill me with the knowledge of Your will in all spiritual wisdom and understanding. My heart's desire is to walk all day today in a manner worthy of You, pleasing You in all respects, bearing fruit for You in everything I do, and increasing in my knowledge of You (Col. 1:10).

"Train yourself for godliness; for while bodily training is of some value, godliness is of value in every way." 1 Timothy 4:7b-8a (ESV)

Your physical heart is a muscle. Therefore—just like your other muscles—it gets stronger and healthier when you exercise. People who don't exercise are almost twice as likely to get heart disease as people who are active (source: webmd.com).

The same principle applies to your spiritual heart as well. In our verse for today, Paul acknowledges the benefits of physical exercise, but then quickly points out that spiritual exercise—training ourselves to be godly—is of far greater value.

The fact is, this battle against sexual impurity isn't a one-time deal, nor is it only for a brief season. We are engaged in this spiritual warfare our entire life. Therefore, we need the endurance of an athlete if we are going to last for the duration and avoid a full enemy takedown.

How then do we exercise toward the goal of being godly? Just like an athlete exercises their muscles through the stress and strain of lifting weights, so we exercise our faith by putting our trust in God through the stress and strain of life. God has commanded us to "be strong and courageous. Do not be frightened, and do not be dismayed," rather, we need to trust in the fact that "the Lord your God is with you wherever you go" (Josh. 1:9 ESV).

We cannot avoid the pull of porn and the lure of lust. It's all around us. But in the middle of those temptations we can exercise our faith in God to help us through. "Those who know (God's) name will trust in (him), for (the) Lord (has) never forsaken those who seek (Him)" (Psa. 9:10). It is only as you "trust in the Lord with all your heart and lean not on your own understanding; in all your ways (acknowledging) him…he will make your paths straight" (Prov. 3:5-6).

If you're anything like me, I'd rather God simply removed the pull of lust and the desires for sinful sexual pleasures. Wouldn't it be nice to never have to struggle with lust ever again? However, if God did do that, I would be more like a weak, sickly couch potato than a trained, strong spiritual athlete. How can I learn to trust in Him fully if I never faced another temptation? How can I rely completely upon Him and say, "You are my God" (Psa. 31:14), if I never pick up my sword and charge into the fray? Exercising myself toward godliness means *not* trusting in what I can do to get myself out of the mess I'm in (Prov. 28:26), but trusting "in the name of the Lord (my) God" (Psa. 20:7).

An athlete exercises and trains for the purpose of building up their strength so that they can endure without faltering. In the same way, we need to learn to "rejoice in our sufferings, knowing that suffering produces endurance, and endurance produces character, and character produces hope" (Rom. 5:3-4 ESV).

Think about this, an athlete doesn't become strong overnight. He exercises for weeks and months on end. In the same way, we must understand that the only way to build our faith in God and our ability to resist temptation in the midst of the battle is to have our faith exercised. It is "with the temptation" that God "will also provide the way of escape, that you may be able to endure it" (1 Cor. 10:13 ESV).

Did you ever stop to consider that even the best athletes don't want to exercise? They have days when the thought of getting off that diet, not doing this particular exercise, ignoring the alarm and sleeping in just this once weighs heavily on their mind. They have to discipline themselves to exercise. They make a choice and commit to keeping at it no matter what.

Are you godly? Do you look like God? Do you act like God? Do you want to be like God (Rom. 8:29; cp. Matt. 10:25; 1 Jn. 2:6; Eph. 5:1)? To become godly and to realize victory in your life over sexual impurity takes training. It takes exercise, building, and discipline. It requires the ability, determination, and know-how to just say "no" to temptation (Titus 2:12), and "a quiet yes to God and he'll be there in no time. Quit dabbling in sin. Purify your inner life. Quit playing the field" (Jas. 4:8 The Message).

If you want to be godly you must faithfully trust in God; you must be a lifetime student of the Bible. You must at all times guard your heart (Prov. 4:23) by watching and reading and listening to things that will promote godliness in your life. You must have quiet time alone with God every day. One day you will see God face to face—will He say to you, "Well done, good and faithful servant" (Matt. 25:21)?

Review, Assess, and Pray:
In the space below, answer the questions. Then, invest five minutes in prayer. Tell God your fears and struggles. Ask Him to open your heart and give you His strength to apply His truth to your life.

1) What did I learn from this?

2) What does God want me to do about it?

THURSDAY - REST
Prayer Time:
Father, as I read today's devotional and study Your Word, please fill me with the knowledge of Your will in all spiritual wisdom and understanding so that I will walk today (and every day) in a manner that glorifies You, pleasing You in all respects, bearing fruit for You in everything I do, and increasing in my knowledge of You (Col. 1:10).

"Come to me, all you who are weary and burdened, and I will give you rest. Take my yoke upon you and learn from me, for I am gentle and humble in heart, and you will find rest for your souls. For my yoke is easy and my burden is light." Matthew 11:28-30

This spiritual battle we are engaged in often leaves us feeling weary, worn, and wiped out. Lamentations 5:5 describes it this way: "Our pursuers are at our necks; we are weary; we are given no rest" (ESV). Have you ever felt that way? I can remember so many times over the years when LuPoMas (see the Introduction) was relentlessly breathing down my neck. I was exhausted, weak, and ready to quit. I felt I couldn't take another step on the battlefield without dropping in utter defeat. I desperately wanted rest, but didn't know how to get it.

Our text for today reminds us that it is only in Christ that we will find our much needed rest (Psa. 62:1). Rest for a Christian comes when we invest consistent time alone with God. The more time we are with our Heavenly Father, the more our spirit is revived. You see, God alone:

> Gives power to the faint, and to him who has no might he increases strength. Even youths shall faint and be weary, and young men shall fall exhausted; but they who wait for the Lord shall renew their strength; they shall mount up with wings like eagles; they shall run and not be weary; they shall walk and not faint. (Isa. 40:29-31 ESV)

I know it can feel this way, but let me assure you that none of us are fighting this battle all-alone. Cling tightly to God's promise, "My presence will go with you, and I will give you rest" (Exod. 33:14 ESV). Stop trying to figure it out on your own. Stop relying on yourself, self-help methods, or the unbiblical advice of others. We've tried those avenues countless times before and they never work. So, what makes us believe this time is the magic bullet? We need to learn to "be still before the Lord and wait patiently for him" (Psa. 37:7) because only He is our "place of quiet retreat" (Psa. 119:114 The Message).

How, then, do we find this rest? Isaiah said that God keeps in perfect peace the man whose mind is steadfast—completely focused upon Him (Isa. 26:3). The rest you and I need is found only in God and is realized only when we place all of our trust and confidence in the God who "gives strength to the weary" (Isa. 40:29 HCSB). Only as you lean fully on the One who "will satisfy the weary soul" (Jer. 31:25 ESV) will you experience a perfect (complete) peace.

As I come to Christ for my strength and help, it is important that I understand,

> The LORD is my shepherd, I shall not be in want. **He** makes me lie down in green pastures, **he** leads me beside quiet waters, **he** restores my soul. **He** guides me in paths of righteousness for his name's sake. Even though I walk through the valley of the shadow of death, I will fear no evil, for **you** are with me; **your** rod and **your** staff, they comfort me. **You** prepare a table before me in the presence of my enemies. **You** anoint my head with oil; my cup overflows. Surely goodness and love will follow me all the days of my life, and I will dwell in the house of the LORD forever. (Psa. 23:1-6, emphasis added)

So the next time you are faced with temptation, the next time you battle with the desire to lust, the next time you struggle with the urge for self-gratification, "Do not be anxious about anything, but in everything, by prayer and petition, with thanksgiving, present your requests to God. And the peace of God, which transcends all understanding, will guard your hearts and your minds in Christ Jesus" (Phil. 4:6-7).

Review, Assess, and Pray:
In the space below, answer the questions. Then, invest five minutes in prayer. Tell God your fears and struggles. Ask Him to open your heart and give you His strength to apply His truth to your life.

1) What did I learn from this?

2) What does God want me to do about it?

Friday – Talk to the Doctor & Take Your Meds

Prayer Time:

Father, thank You so much for Your Word. Thank You for the things You've been teaching me. As I study Scripture today, I ask that You fill me with the knowledge of Your will in all spiritual wisdom and understanding so that I will walk all day in a manner worthy of You, pleasing You in all respects, bearing fruit for You in everything I do, and increasing in my knowledge of You (Col. 1:10).

"Be not wise in your own eyes; fear the LORD and turn away from evil. It will be healing to your flesh and refreshment to your bones."
Proverbs 3:7-8 (ESV)

After having a heart transplant, the recipient starts taking a regimen of medications vital to the health of their new heart. There are drugs that prevent the immune system from making cells that can reject the heart and there are drugs that help control blood pressure, slow down the thickening and narrowing process of the blood vessels of the heart, and decrease the potential for inflammation or swelling (source: hearttransplant.com).

In the same way, your spiritual heart needs certain things in order to keep it (and you) spiritually healthy. God says, "A cheerful heart is good medicine, but a crushed spirit dries up the bones" (Prov. 17:22). Let's face it; unconfessed sin does not make a cheerful heart! King David shared, "When I kept silent"—in other words, when I refused to confess my sin—"my bones wasted away through my groaning all day long. For day and night your hand was heavy upon me; my strength was dried up as by the heat of summer" (Psa. 32:3-4 ESV).

So the first thing you must do to maintain a healthy heart is to go to God with your sin, confess it before Him, agreeing that it is an offense to Him, and claim the forgiveness He offers. Keep a short account with your Maker, Father, Savior, and Friend. You see, "Whoever conceals his transgressions will not prosper, but he who confesses and forsakes them will obtain mercy" (Prov. 28:13 ESV).

Oh, my friend, do not be like the people of Israel who "did secretly against the Lord their God things that were not right" (2 Ki. 17:9 ESV). We battle with the temptation to keep our sexual impurity from others. We even struggle with the desire to keep it from God. Take a cue from David and don't keep it hidden. Rather, "make confession to the Lord ... and do his will. Separate yourselves" from sexual impurity (Ezra 10:11 ESV; cp. 1 Cor. 6:18; 10:14; 2 Tim. 2:22). Confess your sin; be sorry for how you have hurt and dishonored your Heavenly Father (Psa. 38:18; cp. Dan. 9:4). Understand that God "is faithful and just to forgive us our sins and to cleanse us from all unrighteousness" (1 Jn. 1:9 ESV). Acknowledge your sin to God, don't cover it up any longer and He will forgive (Psa. 32:5).

When you visit your doctor, he typically gives you a prescription for what ails you. You are expected to follow it completely—take all your meds at the times and in the way prescribed. If you don't, you shouldn't be surprised when you don't get better. Deuteronomy 7:12-15 says, "If you pay attention to these laws and are careful to follow them,"—in other words, take your meds at the prescribed times and in the prescribed way—"then the LORD your God will keep his covenant of love with you, as he swore to your forefathers. He will love you and bless you ... The LORD will keep you free from every disease."

Sometimes taking your meds can be annoying, especially when you have to take it every four hours and you don't like the taste. I'll never forget as a child, hating the taste of my medicine, so I was glad when the manufacturers started improving the flavor. Admittedly, there are times when we may not like the prescription God gives us. Isn't it a relief to know that God's "words are a honeycomb, sweet to the soul and healing to the bones" (Prov. 16:24)!

Just like a parent lovingly urges their child to buck up and take it anyway, God says, "My son, pay attention to what I say; listen closely to my words. Do not let them out of your sight, keep them within your heart; for they are life to those who find them and health to a man's whole body" (Prov. 4:20-22). In other words, take your meds, do what the doctor tells you to do, and you will get better. Guaranteed!

"If you listen carefully to the voice of the LORD your God and do what is right in his eyes, if you pay attention to his commands and keep all his decrees, I will not bring on you any of the diseases I brought on the Egyptians, for I am the LORD, who heals you" (Exod. 15:26).

Never lose sight of the fact that God wants you to be happy and healthy. He wants you to know genuine, lasting victory over lust, porn, masturbation, and every other form of sexual impurity. And so I echo the words of John: "Dear friend, I pray that you may enjoy good health and that all may go well with you, even as your soul is getting along well" (3 Jn. 1:2).

Just as the doctor tells you to take two aspirin and call him in the morning—so you and I need to read God's Word daily and talk to Him every morning.

Review, Assess, and Pray:
In the space below, answer the questions. Then, invest five minutes in prayer. Tell God your fears and struggles. Ask Him to open your heart and give you His strength to apply His truth to your life.

1) What did I learn from this?

2) What does God want me to do about it?

SATURDAY – SEE YOUR DOCTOR REGULARLY
Prayer Time:
Another week has come and gone. How are you doing? What have been your struggles as you've been working your way through this book? Have you talked with your accountability partner about it? Are you continuing to meet? Are you praying for each other?

Father, fill me right now with the knowledge of Your will in all spiritual wisdom and understanding so that I will walk today in a manner worthy of You, pleasing You in all respects, bearing fruit for You in everything I do, and increasing in my knowledge of You (Col. 1:10).

_____

"And now I commend you to God and to the word of his grace, which is able to build you up and to give you the inheritance among all those who are sanctified." Acts 20:32 (ESV)

After a heart transplant, the recipient must see their physician regularly. These routine health exams and tests not only make sure the heart is functioning properly, but they enable the doctor to discover problems early, when your chances for treatment and cure are better.

Do you want to be spiritually healthy? Do you want to prevent sexual impurity from permeating every aspect of your life, dominating your thoughts, and dictating your actions? If so, what are you doing right now to avoid it? Are you seeing your Great Physician on a regular basis?

Jesus made it abundantly clear that our top priority must be the kingship of God in our heart as we live out His righteousness in our life (Matt. 6:33). To do that, we need to invest time with God daily.

Here we are at the end of week four of this devotional guide. Each and every day we have opened our Bible and learned from the Holy Spirit. Daily you have had to face some things in your life and make some critical decisions. It is my prayer that this has already been a blessing to you. However, once you've completed this devotional guide, what's next? Might I suggest that you start this book all over again with Week 1? There is so much to be learned and applied within these pages. No matter what, I challenge you to continue to dive into Scripture to seek God's face?

Studying God's Word can help you see potential problems in your life before they start. A daily quiet time with God can also help you find a problem that is already beginning to develop in your life. Let's face it though; devotions are often hard to do.

We tend to get so busy and face so many demands on our time that we can easily push any alone time with God right out of our daily routine. So, let me ask you a question here: Do you love Jesus? "Well of course I do!" you exclaim. Great! Does it make sense then that you should invest regular time with Him and get to know Him much deeper than you already do?

Jesus said, "If you love me, you will keep my commandments" (Jn. 14:15 ESV). My love for Christ should prompt my obedience to Christ. I cannot walk in obedience to Him and I cannot know what it is He wants me to do if I am not reading His Word to find out!

Do you want real, lasting victory over sexual impurity in your life? God says, "If you will listen to all that I command you, and will walk in my ways, and do what is right in my eyes by keeping my statutes and my commandments ... I will be with you and will build you a sure house" (1 Ki. 11:38 ESV). I see that as a promise I can take to the bank! As I seek His face—as I search the Scriptures to learn more of who He is and what His will is—and then I immediately choose to obey, He will show me what real victory and freedom is like!

God's desire for you is that you would have "such a heart as this always, to fear (God) and to keep all (His) commandments, that it might go well with (you)" (Deut. 5:29 ESV). That will not happen if you do not "turn from your evil ways and keep (God's) commandments and (God's) statutes" (2 Ki. 17:13 ESV). So I want to challenge you—right here, right now—cry out against porn, lust, and masturbation and say "depart from me, you evil doers, that I may keep the commandments of my God" (Psa. 119:115 ESV)!

King David declared of God, "You make known to me the path of life; in your presence there is fullness of joy; at your right hand are pleasures forevermore" (Psa. 16:11 ESV). Meeting with God on a regular basis is the foundation for a joyful life. Satan knows this and uses all means at his disposal to chip away at our relationship with God. One of his most successful tactics has been to make us so busy that we feel we just don't have the time to invest alone with the Lord.

So let me close out this week with the following verses:

> "Blessed are those whose way is blameless, who walk in the law of the Lord! Blessed are those who keep his testimonies, who seek him with their whole heart, who also do no wrong, but walk in his ways! You have commanded your precepts to be kept diligently. Oh that my ways may be steadfast in keeping your statutes! Then I shall not be put to shame, having my eyes fixed on all your commandments. I will praise you with an

upright heart, when I learn of your righteous rules. I will keep your statutes." (Psa. 119:1-8a ESV)

Review, Assess, and Pray:
In the space below, answer the questions. Then, invest five minutes in prayer. Tell God your fears and struggles. Ask Him to open your heart and give you His strength to apply His truth to your life.

1) What did I learn from this?

2) What does God want me to do about it?

Authentic Accountability

This is an important time to share with your accountability partner. Both of you, discuss these questions in detail. Challenge each other, be honest with each other, pray for each other, and don't be afraid to get into each other's lives. Be intentional, be real, and be ready for a blessing.

1. What did you learn from this week's set of devotions?

2. What changes need to take place in your life because of this?

3. What steps of faith are you taking to make those changes?

4. Select at least one verse from this week to memorize. Explain why you chose that verse and how it applies to you.

WEEK FIVE
This is War

We have begun week five and I'm willing to bet that if you have been staying with this faithfully, you are feeling the relentless attacks of the enemy on your heart and mind. We are at war my friend—of that let there be no doubt. How are you doing? Seriously—how is the battle going?

As we work through the devotionals of this week, our focus is going to be on the spiritual warfare we are engaged in. Remember, we are not fighting against men; our battle is against the evil of hell itself (Eph. 6:12). You see, just as Satan deceived Eve by his cunning, his goal is to lead your thoughts away from being fully devoted to Christ (2 Cor. 11:3). He knows that what you think determines what you do (Prov. 27:19).

At times this war can seem to be overwhelming. I love God's promise that "when you go out to war against your enemies (against sexual impurity), and see horses and chariots and an army larger than your own, you shall not be afraid of them, for the LORD your God is with you, who brought you up out of the land of Egypt" (Deut. 20:1 ESV, addition mine). God has delivered you out of the very pit of hell itself. He has adopted you as His child (Eph. 1:5; cp. Jn. 1:12; Gal. 4:5-6; Rom. 8:15-17) and given you a glorious inheritance (Tit. 3:7). Do you really think He is going to let you flounder and be massacred by the enemy (Deut. 31:6, 8; 1 Chron. 28:20; Psa. 37:28; 94:14)?

For so many years I let myself be defeated. I stayed stuck in the mire of my sin, thinking that there was no way out. I was wrong (1 Cor. 10:13). Today, praise God, I am free! All because "the Lord stood by me and strengthened me, so that through me the message might be fully proclaimed...I was rescued from the lion's mouth. The Lord will rescue me (and you) from every evil deed and bring me (and you) safely into his heavenly kingdom" (2 Tim. 4:17-18 ESV, additions mine).

This war can feel defeating at times—believe me, I know. Keep in mind:

> That neither death nor life, nor angels nor rulers, nor things present nor things to come, nor powers, nor height nor depth, nor anything else in all creation (including lust, porn, and masturbation), will be able to separate us from the love of God in Christ Jesus our Lord" (Rom. 8:38-39 ESV, addition mine).

That's powerful!

You will struggle from time to time with feelings of discouragement and thoughts like, "Will I ever be free?" Here is a verse that has been a great encouragement to me: "Be strong and courageous. Do not fear or be in dread...for it is the Lord your God who goes with you. He will not leave you or forsake you" (Deut. 31:6 ESV).

Let me encourage you to "lay aside every weight, and the sin which clings so closely, and ... run with endurance the race that is set before (you)" (Heb. 12:1 ESV). This battle will never be easy. In fact, "in your struggle against sin you have not yet resisted to the point of shedding your blood" (Heb. 12:4 ESV). There are still rough times ahead. As you face each struggle, never lose sight of the fact that God "has delivered us from the domain of darkness and transferred us to the kingdom of his beloved Son" (Col. 1:13 ESV).

You can fight this and win! You can do it through Christ because He will give you the strength and He will supply every need of yours according to His riches (Phil. 4:13, 19)!

SUNDAY – SUPERFICIAL SACRIFICES
Prayer Time:
Father, as I join my brothers and sisters in worship of You and the study of Your Word, please fill me with the knowledge of Your will in all spiritual wisdom and understanding. It is my desire that I walk

throughout this day in a manner worthy of You, pleasing You in all respects, bearing fruit for You in everything I do, and increasing in my knowledge of You (Col. 1:10).

"Your burnt offerings are not acceptable; your sacrifices do not please me." (Jeremiah 6:20b)

Ouch! Those words sting, or at least they should. I certainly want my worship of God to be pleasing to Him, don't you? So when my Heavenly Father says to me, "Your worship of me is not acceptable—it doesn't please me," I should feel cut to the quick. It should drive me to want to make it right so that my life truly honors and glorifies the One who died for me.

Since today is a day we typically set aside for worship, I challenge you to be asking the very serious question: Will my worship be acceptable to God?

Going to church should never be about me. It's not about what blessing I get from the music, or how many people acknowledge that I'm there. It's not about how great the message was or how on-fire the preacher seemed to be. It's definitely not about any "warm fuzzies" we might walk away with. Going to church must be all about God, for He is why we are there!

If I attend for the purpose of receiving a blessing, if I expect to walk away encouraged, or if I am discouraged because I don't leave feeling better than when I arrived, then I act like it's all about me. I am there to worship self. That's not church. That's not Christianity it's religion —and God isn't about religion.

If you walk into church today and participate in what we often call a "worship service" yet your heart is full of unconfessed sin, God says:

> I hate, I despise your religious feasts; I cannot stand your assemblies. Even though you bring me burnt offerings and grain offerings, I will not accept them. Though you bring choice fellowship offerings, I will have no regard for them. Away with the noise of your songs! I will not listen to the music of your harps....You have lifted up the shrine of your king, the pedestal

of your idols, the star of your god—which you made for yourselves. (Amos 5:21-23, 26)

Simply put, until God has highest value and Jesus is the center of our universe, we won't be able to get rid of our idols, and anything we say or do in "worship" of Him is an affront to our Savior and is ultimately meaningless.

As you invest time today in going to church and joining with other believers in praise to our Heavenly Father, I want to urge you to carefully consider what He thinks of your worship. When you harbor sin in your heart, God's not interested in the fact that you are singing the songs at the top of your lungs. He's not impressed when you bow your head or raise your hands in worship. His heart doesn't skip a beat as you place money in the offering plate. He's not nodding in approval when you open your Bible as the preacher brings the message. Those things mean nothing to Him if your heart is not right with Him (1 Sam. 16:7).

Before the service begins, take time to bow before the Almighty in prayer. Ask Him to search and know your heart. Tell Him you want Him to test you thoroughly and reveal your deepest thoughts so that you can lay your sin before Him (Psa. 139:23-24; cp. Psa. 26:2). Keep in mind that "the Lord detests the sacrifice of the wicked, but the prayer of the upright pleases him" (Prov. 15:8).

Let me close out today's thoughts with this passage from Isaiah 1:11-17a.

> "The multitude of your sacrifices—what are they to me?" says the Lord. "I have more than enough of burnt offerings, of rams and the fat of fattened animals; I have no pleasure in the blood of bulls and lambs and goats. When you come to appear before me, who has asked this of you, this trampling of my courts? Stop bringing meaningless offerings! Your incense is detestable to me. New Moons, Sabbaths and convocations—I cannot bear your evil assemblies. Your New Moon festivals and your appointed feasts my soul hates. They have become a burden to me; I am weary of bearing them. When you spread out your hands in prayer, I will hide my eyes from you; even if you offer many prayers, I will not listen. Your hands are full of blood;

wash and make yourselves clean. Take your evil deeds out of my sight! Stop doing wrong, learn to do right!"

Review, Assess, and Pray:
In the space below, answer the questions. Then, invest five minutes in prayer. Tell God your fears and struggles. Ask Him to open your heart and give you His strength to apply His truth to your life.

1) What did I learn from this?

2) What does God want me to do about it?

MONDAY – THE BATTLE BELONGS TO WHO?
Prayer Time:
Father, I desperately need the knowledge of Your will in all spiritual wisdom and understanding, only then will I walk in a manner worthy of You, pleasing You in all respects, bearing fruit for You in everything I do, and increasing in my knowledge of You (Col. 1:10).

"Today you are drawing near for battle against your enemies: let not your heart faint. Do not fear or panic or be in dread of them, for the LORD your God is he who goes with you to fight for you against your enemies, to give you the victory." Deuteronomy 20:3-4 (ESV)

In this battle against lust, porn, and masturbation (along with any other form of sexual impurity), have you ever felt like tiny little David up against big and mighty Goliath? Do you remember how that story ended (see 1 Samuel 17:40-54)? Consider this: Is God any different today than He was then? The God who was with David in that epic battle is the same God who is with you right now (Heb. 13:8; Mal. 3:6; Jas. 1:17; and Psa. 90:2). The same power that He gave to David to defeat that giant in his life, He makes available to you right now to combat yours (2 Pet. 1:3; I Samuel 17:47).

God has promised to give you everything you need to fight this battle (Phil. 4:19). Victory isn't something *you* have to manufacture. Hey, we've tried that in the past and failed miserably. That's why we end up feeling so discouraged and defeated. When you and I try to beat this beast in our own strength, we will lose every time. Scripture doesn't say, "You are from great stock, for greater are you than he that is in the world;" it says, "You are from God and have overcome them, for he who is in you is greater than he who is in the world" (1 Jn. 4:4 ESV).

We read in 2 Samuel 22:

> David spoke to the Lord the words of this song on the day when the LORD delivered him from the hand of all his enemies, and from the hand of Saul. He said, 'The LORD is my rock and my fortress and my deliverer, my God, my rock, in whom I take refuge, my shield, and the horn of my salvation, my stronghold and my refuge, my savior…I call upon the LORD, who is worthy to be praised, and I am saved from my enemies. (2 Sam. 22:1-4 ESV)

Later on in that same chapter, David said that God is the one who equipped him with the strength he needed to fight the battle and win (2 Sam. 22:40).

Look at what God tells Joshua. "Have I not commanded you? Be strong and courageous. Do not be frightened, and do not be dismayed, for the LORD your God is with you wherever you go" (Josh. 1:9 ESV). My friend, we truly can do all things through Christ who gives us His strength (Phil. 4:8)! This is because it is "through (God) we push down our foes; through (His) name we tread down those who rise up against us" (Psa. 44:5 ESV).

I can vividly remember, as a five year old boy, being terrified because I had wandered too close to a bees nest. They were unhappy about my presence and began actively buzzing around my head. I stood there, literally frozen in place, frightened and crying. Then I heard my dad's soft voice saying, "Son, it's going to be alright. Look at me." Too scared to open my eyes I whimpered, "No." "Son, look – at – me." Slowly I opened my eyes to see dad standing just a few feet away.

He smiled, held out his hands and said, "Now, slowly walk toward me." I squeezed my eyes shut and began trembling. "I can't," I whined. "Do you trust me?" he asked. I slowly nodded my head. "Then look at me, and begin to walk toward me."

Reluctantly I took a tentative step toward him, never taking my eyes off of him. Nothing happened. The bees didn't go ballistic and suddenly bombard with stingers, so I took another step. And then another. Again and again until I was wrapped in my father's loving embrace.

As I think back on that event, I am reminded of Psalm 118:12-13 which says, "They surrounded me like bees; they went out like a fire among thorns; in the name of the LORD I cut them off! I was pushed hard, so that I was falling, but the LORD helped me" (ESV). Can you relate? Would you say that at times the temptations for sexual impurity surround you like bees and poke you like fiery thorns? Have you ever felt like they were pushing you so hard that you were falling? God is there to help you. Through His strength you can cut them off!

Invest the time today to read these verses: Deuteronomy 28:7; 2 Chronicles 32:7-8; 2 Kings 6:15-17; Psalm 138:3; Isaiah 40:31; 41:10; 54:17; Luke 1:37; Romans 8:37-39 and Ephesians 6:10-13.

Review, Assess, and Pray:
In the space below, answer the questions. Then, invest five minutes in prayer. Tell God your fears and struggles. Ask Him to open your heart and give you His strength to apply His truth to your life.

1) What did I learn from this?

2) What does God want me to do about it?

TUESDAY – JUST SAY NO!

Prayer Time:

Father, You are hitting me hard this week and it's only Tuesday! Thank you. Please fill me with the knowledge of Your will in all spiritual wisdom and understanding so that I will walk today in a manner worthy of You, pleasing You in all respects, bearing fruit for You in everything I do, and increasing in my knowledge of You (Col. 1:10).

"For the grace of God that brings salvation has appeared to all men. It teaches us to say 'No' to ungodliness and worldly passions, and to live self-controlled, upright, and godly lives in the present age." Titus 2:11-12

If you can remember back to the Ronald Regan era, you may recall that our president's wife, Nancy Reagan, spearheaded an anti-drug campaign entitled, "Just Say No." It began when the first lady was visiting the Longfellow Elementary School in Oakland, California. She was asked by a schoolgirl what to do if she was offered drugs. Mrs. Regan responded by saying, "Just say 'No!'" and it stuck!

As we see in our verse for today, the amazing grace of God teaches us that when faced with the temptation to give in to lust we need to just say "No." Don't play around with it. In fact, don't even think about how to gratify the sinful desires of the flesh (Rom. 13:14). Instead, "renounce secret and shameful ways; ... do not use deception, nor ... distort the word of God" (2 Cor. 4:1-2). "And give no opportunity to the devil" (Eph. 4:27 ESV).

Why is it so important to just say "No"? "If you live according to the flesh you will die, but if by the Spirit you put to death the deeds of the body (just saying "No"), you will live" (Rom. 8:13 ESV, addition mine). You see, "those who live according to the flesh set their minds on the things of the flesh, but those who (just say "No" and) live according to the Spirit set their minds on the things of the Spirit" (Rom. 8:5 ESV, addition mine).

To just say "No" means you are putting "to death therefore what is earthly in you: sexual immorality, impurity, passion, evil desire, and covetousness, which is idolatry" (Col. 3:5 ESV). It means you are

90

learning how to "discipline (your) body and keep it under control, lest …(you) should be disqualified" (1 Cor. 9:27 ESV).

Saying "No" to sexual impurity, and choosing to live a self-controlled, upright, and godly life is a daily decision you have to make. Not just when you get up in the morning, but all the time. Every instance where you are faced with a temptation, you are also faced with a decision. Do I give in this time or do I continue to stand firm and fight it? Do I yield to the Spirit and glorify God, or do I focus on self and give in to my fleshly desires?

We are constantly using our mind throughout each day to make decisions. This is why it's vital that we discipline our mind to just say "No" to the cries of the flesh for sinful pleasure and "Yes" to the promptings of the Holy Spirit for purity.

Sounds great—just say "No." How do we say "No"? I mean, when I am tempted it's not usually in a place where I can shout out at the top of my lungs, "NO way, Satan. I won't do that!" That would probably warrant a few unwanted stares and create some uncomfortable situations. So how do we say "No" to temptation when it slams into us? I believe we need to ask Jesus that question. After all, He faced every kind of temptation known to man and came out victorious (Heb. 4:15). Please take a moment to read Matthew 4:1-11.

If you just read that passage in Matthew 4, you should be able to easily answer this next question: How did Jesus just say "No"? How did He respond to each and every temptation? He simply said, "It is written…," and then quoted Scripture. How well do you know your Bible? When faced with the temptation to lust, or to look at porn, or to masturbate while fantasizing, what Scripture can you quote so that you can take captive those thoughts and make them obedient to Christ (2 Cor. 10:5)?

I find it so encouraging that Jesus did not use His divine power to defeat Satan. He provided an example by using the same weapon that we have available to us today, namely, the Word of God. It is as you hide God's Word in your heart that you will be victorious over your temptations (Psa. 119:11). It is also when you choose to do what God's Word says that you will be a pure man (Psa. 119:9).

Also notice that Satan could not counter the truth of God's Word. Every time Jesus quoted scripture, Satan was finished with that particular temptation. His lies can never stand up against God's absolute truth. We are commanded to "Resist the devil, and he will flee from you" (Jas. 4:7).

Just say "No," my friend. We are able to resist temptation the same way Jesus did, with Scripture. If you are going to defeat Satan's attacks on your mind with his deceitful lies, you must depend upon the Word of God.

Review, Assess, and Pray:
In the space below, answer the questions. Then, invest five minutes in prayer. Tell God your fears and struggles. Ask Him to open your heart and give you His strength to apply His truth to your life.

1) What did I learn from this?

2) What does God want me to do about it?

WEDNESDAY – MORE THAN A CONQUEROR, AN OVERCOMER
Prayer Time:
Father, as I am seeking You, please fill me with the knowledge of Your will in all spiritual wisdom and understanding so that I will walk today in a manner worthy of You, pleasing You in all respects, bearing fruit for You in everything I do, and increasing in my knowledge of You (Col. 1:10).

_____

"No, in all these things we are more than conquerors through him who loved us." Romans 8:37

I like that phrase, "more than conquerors." It is filled with so much power and encouragement. It means that we haven't just won a battle; we've won the war! In the Greek, that phrase means to over-conquer, to win with success to spare, to be supremely victorious. Isn't that great?

So, why do we have times when we feel less than a conqueror? Why do we struggle with feelings of defeat and discouragement, especially when we've given in—yet again—to our temptation? It's because we don't yet fully understand what it means to be a conqueror. So let's look at the steps we need to take to win with "success to spare."

1. Understand you can't win on your own. Look again at our verse for today. We are more than conquerors only through the power Christ gives us (cp. Phil. 4:13). He gives us that power (see 2 Pet. 1:3) not because of anything we have done, or are capable of doing, but simply because of His amazing love for us.

Let this truth sink deep into your heart. You will win the war against lust, porn, and masturbation because "You are from God and have overcome … for he who is in you is greater than he who is in the world" (1 Jn. 4:4 ESV). You will be victorious over sexual impurity only because "God is able to make all grace abound to you, so that having all sufficiency in all things at all times, you may abound in every good work" (2 Cor. 9:8 ESV).

On my own I will fail. But we're not on our own. "What then shall we say to these things? If God is for us, who can be against us" (Rom. 8:31 ESV)? Never lose sight of the truth that "according to the riches of his glory he (grants) you to be strengthened with power through his Spirit in your inner being" (Eph. 3:16 ESV).

2. You must believe He has a plan. Paul assures us that "all things work together for good" (Rom. 8:28 ESV). You aren't doing that work, God is. "For it is God who works in you, both to will and to work for his good pleasure" (Phil. 2:13 ESV). Never forget that it is God "who is able to do far more abundantly than all that we ask or think, according to the power at work within us" (Eph. 3:20 ESV).

93

We keep talking about God's power. Just think about the power that is at work within you. Our God is the Almighty, most Holy, Sovereign God of the universe! He has the power to create out of nothing (see Genesis 1). He can part water, move mountains, heal the sick, and raise the dead. God can do anything (see Matt. 19:26; Mark 9:23; 10:27; Luke 1:37 and Jer. 32:17 for example).

Now, as you begin to realize His limitless, infinite power, consider this: "I know the plans I have for you, declares the Lord, plans for welfare and not for evil, to give you a future and a hope" (Jer. 29:11 ESV). God has a plan for your life. A plan for your good (Rom. 8:28). Sometimes we struggle with accepting that, let alone understanding it. But then, we will never be able to fully grasp it because God's thoughts are not like our thoughts, and His ways are far beyond anything we could ever imagine (Isa. 55:8-9).

So, when you are feeling defeated and you are discouraged because you let your guard down and momentarily fell on the battlefield, remember God's plan and God's power at work in your life. And then:

3. Pray! Invest time on your knees talking with your Heavenly Father. Tell Him your frustrations, your fears, and admit your failures. Cry out to Him from your broken heart. "The Lord is near to the brokenhearted and saves the crushed in spirit" (Psa. 34:18 ESV).

To know victory, talk to the Victor! To be able to overcome, invest time with the Overcomer! "Cast your cares on the LORD and he will sustain you; he will never let the righteous fall" (Psa. 55:22).

4. Make the right choices. "Do not enter the path of the wicked, and do not walk in the way of the evil. Avoid it; do not go on it; turn away from it and pass on" (Prov. 4:14-15 ESV).

Daily choose:

To put off your old self, which belongs to your former manner of life and is corrupt through deceitful desires, and to be renewed in the spirit of your minds, and to put on the new self, created

94

after the likeness of God in true righteousness and holiness. Give no opportunity to the devil. (Eph. 4:22-24, 27 ESV)

"Take no part in the unfruitful works of darkness" (Eph. 5:11 ESV).

Let's close with this thought from James 4:7—"Submit yourselves therefore to God. Resist the devil, and he will flee from you" (ESV).

Review, Assess, and Pray:
In the space below, answer the questions. Then, invest five minutes in prayer. Tell God your fears and struggles. Ask Him to open your heart and give you His strength to apply His truth to your life.

1) What did I learn from this?

2) What does God want me to do about it?

THURSDAY – HOW TO BE SUCCESSFULLY PROSPEROUS
Prayer Time:
Take a moment before you begin today and ask God to reveal Himself to you, to soften your heart to receive what He wants to tell you, and to give you the strength to apply it to your life.

Father, fill me with the knowledge of Your will in all spiritual wisdom and understanding so that I will walk today in a manner worthy of You, pleasing You in all respects, bearing fruit for You in everything I do, and increasing in my knowledge of You (Col. 1:10).

———————————

"But seek first the kingdom of God and his righteousness, and all these things will be added to you." Matthew 6:33 (ESV)

It is probably a safe assumption that you want to be successful and prosperous, whether it's at work, in your financial endeavors, or in your relationships with others, and so on. That's not necessarily a bad thing. However, we must keep in mind that prosperity and success, as the world defines it, is not our primary goal.

The top priority in your life must be to know God and to honor and glorify Him with every aspect of your life (1 Cor. 10:31; Col. 3:17). So, ask yourself two important questions. First, "What is most important to me?" You can tell the answer to that by looking at two things: your checkbook (Where do you spend most of your money?) and your clock/calendar (Where do you spend most of your time outside of work?). Second, "What drives me throughout the day?" In other words, "What do I get excited and passionate about?"

Your answer to those two questions will say much about where your priorities lie. If you are putting your emphasis on anything other than glorifying God and knowing Him, you will fail to achieve your ultimate goal.

Read our verse for today again. Consider carefully what Jesus is saying. First and foremost, the things we are to seek after are God's kingdom and God's righteousness in our lives. It is kind of hard to do that when self is sitting on the throne. When we are trying to build our own little kingdoms, seeking a different "king" to reign in our lives is low priority.

We tend to put self on the throne daily. We try to manufacture events and control circumstances in such a way that we are able to experience constant happiness and satisfaction. As a result, we become a slave to self—all thoughts and energies being directed toward fulfilling the will of "King Me." We need to learn how to say, along with Paul, "I do not account my life of any value nor as precious to myself, if only I may finish my course and the ministry that I received from the Lord Jesus, to testify to the gospel of the grace of God" (Acts 20:24 ESV).

The word Jesus used for "seeking" Him first, carries the idea of craving something so much that you focus all of your thought and attention on finding it, so as to acquire it. It's like a heat-seeking missile that, when fired, has a singular target or goal and won't stop until it reaches it. Nothing can deter it from its purpose. Just like that missile, we are to seek after God's kingdom and righteousness to reign in our life. In other words, we should be seeking it at any cost—bending our entire will toward pursuing and laying hold of it.

Seeking first God's kingdom and righteousness means this: You are denying your selfish desires while craving after and pursuing His rule, His will, and His authority in every aspect of your life—both public and private. Seeking God's kingdom and righteousness involves completely immersing yourself in the understanding of His will, and walking in total obedience to God at all times.

Before being prosperous and successful in any other endeavor, you should desire—more than anything—to be prosperous and successful as a Christian. Only as you seek God's kingdom and righteousness first in your life will you experience true prosperity and success.

Seeking God first in your life begins as you study and meditate on God's Word. God instructed Joshua that "this Book of the Law shall not depart from your mouth, but you shall meditate on it day and night, so that you may be careful to do according to all that is written in it. For then you will make your way prosperous, and then you will have good success" (Josh. 1:8 ESV).

So, to be successfully prosperous, we are to open our Bible and "read in it all the days of (our) life, that (we) may learn to fear the LORD (our) God by keeping all the words of this law and these statutes, and doing them" (Deut. 17:19 ESV). Our challenge for today is to "delight ... in the law of the LORD, and on his law ... meditate day and night. (Then we will be) like a tree planted by streams of water that yields its fruit in its season, and its leaf does not wither. In all that (we do), (we will) prosper" (Psa. 1:2-3 ESV).

Review, Assess, and Pray:
In the space below, answer the questions. Then, invest five minutes in prayer. Tell God your fears and struggles. Ask Him to open your heart and give you His strength to apply His truth to your life.

1) What did I learn from this?

2) What does God want me to do about it?

FRIDAY - RESCUED
Prayer Time:
Take a moment before you begin today and ask God to reveal Himself to you, to soften your heart to receive what He wants to tell you, and to give you the strength to apply it to your life.

Father, fill me with the knowledge of Your will in all spiritual wisdom and understanding so that I will walk today in a manner worthy of You, pleasing You in all respects, bearing fruit for You in everything I do, and increasing in my knowledge of You (Col. 1:10).

Today's devotional is going to be a bit different. Satan wants nothing more than for you to stay defeated—even though you have already won the victory through Christ. The enemy of your soul wants you to believe you can't beat this beast. Think about when he tempted Christ in the wilderness (Matt. 4:1-11 and Luke 4:1-13). How did Jesus defeat each temptation? With Scripture! So, for the rest of this devotional, I want you to focus on what God has to say about your deliverance. Be sure to talk with your accountability partner about how these truths apply to you.

"Our God is a God of salvation, and to God, the Lord, belong deliverances from death" (Psa. 68:20 ESV).

God will "Rescue the weak and the needy; deliver them from the hand of the wicked" (Psa. 82:4 ESV)

Just before being thrown into the fiery furnace, Shadrach, Meshach, and Abednego said, "Our God whom we serve is able to deliver us from the burning fiery furnace, and he will deliver us out of your hand, O king. But if not, be it known to you, O king, that we will not serve your gods or worship the golden image that you have set up" (Dan. 3:17-18). Their God is our God! God is able to deliver us from bondage to lust, porn, and masturbation! But even if He didn't, we must determine that we will never serve those gods.

God stands ready to "deliver (your) soul from death, yes, (your) feet from falling." Why? "That (you) may walk before God in the light of life" (Psa. 56:13 ESV).

What an honor to "say of the Lord, 'He is my refuge and my fortress, my God, in whom I trust'" (Psa. 91:2)!

Truly we can say to God, "You are a hiding place for me; you preserve me from trouble; you surround me with shouts of deliverance" (Psa. 32:7 ESV).

"The Lord will rescue me from every evil deed and bring me safely into his heavenly kingdom. To him be the glory forever and ever. Amen" (2 Tim. 4:18 ESV). Do you believe that?

"The LORD is my rock and my fortress and my deliverer, my God, my rock, in whom I take refuge, my shield, and the horn of my salvation, my stronghold" (Psa. 18:2 ESV).

"As for me, I am poor and needy, but the Lord takes thought for me. You are my help and my deliverer; do not delay, O my God" (Psa. 40:17 ESV)! Isn't it great to know that even though we don't have the strength, ability, or resources on our own to win this fight against sexual impurity, God is our help and deliverer!

I challenge you to make this your daily prayer: "Rescue me, O my God, from the hand of the wicked, from the grasp of the unjust and cruel man" (Psa. 71:4 ESV). Why? Because only God can rescue us from the iron grip that sexual impurity holds us in.

Let's conclude today with this wonderful promise: "Call upon me in the day of trouble; I will deliver you, and you shall glorify me" (Psa. 50:15 ESV)!

Review, Assess, and Pray:
In the space below, answer the questions. Then, invest five minutes in prayer. Tell God your fears and struggles. Ask Him to open your heart and give you His strength to apply His truth to your life.

1) What did I learn from this?

2) What does God want me to do about it?

SATURDAY – MY DECLARATION OF WAR
Prayer Time:
Father, fill me with the knowledge of Your will in all spiritual wisdom and understanding so that I will walk today in a manner worthy of You, pleasing You in all respects, bearing fruit for You in everything I do, and increasing in my knowledge of You (Col. 1:10).

"For we do not wrestle against flesh and blood, but against the rulers, against the authorities, against the cosmic powers over this present darkness, against the spiritual forces of evil in the heavenly places." Ephesians 6:12

The last five weeks have been intense. Have you felt it? Our spiritual foe does not want us to be pure men. He does not want us realizing the victory that God has promised us. He wants us to live in defeat. We are at war, gentlemen. But understand: This is a war you can win!

"Thanks be to God, who gives us the victory through our Lord Jesus Christ" (1 Cor. 15:57 ESV). "No, in all these things we are more than conquerors through him who loved us" (Rom. 8:37 ESV). So, again I say, "thanks be to God, who in Christ always leads us in triumphal procession" (2 Cor. 2:14 ESV)! Why? Because we "can do all things through him who strengthens" us (Phil. 4:13 ESV).

It's a powerful thing to understand that "sin will have no dominion over you" (Rom. 6:14 ESV) because of God's grace. This is because not "height nor depth, nor anything else in all creation (including lust, porn, and masturbation), will be able to separate us from the love of God in Christ Jesus our Lord" (Rom. 8:39 ESV, addition mine). "For the Lord your God is he who goes with you to fight for you against your enemies, to give you the victory" (Deut. 20:4 ESV).

I want to close with this thought. For the last five weeks we have been studying God's Word. If you are "a hearer of the word and not a doer," God says you are:

> Like a man who looks intently at his natural face in a mirror. For he looks at himself and goes away and at once forgets what he was like. But the one who looks into the perfect law, the law of liberty, and perseveres, being no hearer who forgets but a

doer who acts, he will be blessed in his doing. (Jas. 1:23-25 ESV)

Be a "doer" guys. Apply what you have learned. That is the only way you will keep yourself pure (Psa. 119:9).

A couple of years ago I decided I needed to write out a document declaring my intent to be a pure man. I searched Scripture and found 15 Biblical principles that I wanted (and needed) to live by. Today that document sits in a frame on my desk in my office as a daily reminder of my commitment to sexual purity—first and foremost to God, second to my wife, third to my family, and finally to myself. I share this with you in the hopes that you, too, will choose to declare war on sexual impurity in your life.

Here is The Pure Man's Declaration of War:

Whereas the truth of God's Word has been opposed, and the execution of His will obstructed in my life: Now, therefore, I, _____, a redeemed child of God, in virtue of the power of the Holy Spirit who in me resides, do hereby formally declare war against impurity and the sinful desires of my flesh which are battling against my soul (1 Pet. 2:11; Jas. 4:1; Gal. 5:17).

In this state of conflict, it is resolved and determined that I will put to death the misdeeds of my body (Rom. 8:13). I therefore do assert and promise before God and the witnesses whose signatures are affixed below that:

- I WILL from this point forward take full responsibility for my thoughts, words, and actions;
- I WILL learn from my mistakes, repent of my sins, and endeavor to be holy in all of my thoughts, words, and actions (Eph. 1:4; 1 Pet. 1:15-16);
- I WILL seek first God's kingdom and righteousness in every aspect of my life (Matt. 6:33);
- I WILL daily (Ac. 17:11) invest my time in the study and meditation of God's Word, turning my ear to God's wisdom and applying my heart to understanding His Truth (Prov. 2:2-3);

- I WILL treasure (Job 23:12) and memorize God's Word, and daily apply its truth and standards to my life (Psa. 119:9, 11, 97, 105), being a doer of the Word and not a hearer only (Jas. 1:25);
- I WILL be a man who always endeavors to walk before God in integrity (1 Ki. 9:4; Psa. 25:21; Prov. 10:9);
- I WILL endeavor to set my mind only on those things that glorify God (Col. 3:2; Phil. 4:8);
- I WILL strive to take captive every thought and make each one fully obedient to Christ (2 Cor. 10:5);
- I WILL daily prepare my mind for battle, I WILL be self-controlled and I WILL set my hope for victory fully on Christ (1 Pet. 1:13);
- I WILL control my own body in a way that is honorable, abstaining from the sinful desires of my flesh (1 Pet. 2:11) and avoiding all forms of sexual immorality (1 Thess. 4:3-4);
- I WILL NOT look lustfully at a woman (Job 31:1; Prov. 6:25; Matt. 5:28);
- I WILL NOT allow even a hint of sexual immorality, or any kind of impurity be in me (Eph. 5:3);
- I WILL NOT allow my TV, computer, or handheld devices, movies, books, magazines, or any other form of entertainment to set before my eyes any ungodly image or standard (Psa. 25:15; 101:2-3; Ezek. 20:7; Num. 33:55; Rom. 16:17; 1 Thess. 5:21-22);
- I WILL always strive to love God with all my heart, with all my soul, with all my mind, and with all my strength (Mark 12:30);
- I WILL fight the good fight, I WILL finish the race, I WILL keep the faith (2 Tim. 4:7).

Review, Assess, and Pray:

In the space below, answer the questions. Then, invest five minutes in prayer. Tell God your fears and struggles. Ask Him to open your heart and give you His strength to apply His truth to your life.

1) What did I learn from this?

2) What does God want me to do about it?

AUTHENTIC ACCOUNTABILITY

This is an important time to share with your accountability partner. Both of you discuss these questions in detail. Challenge each other, be honest with each other, pray for each other, and don't be afraid to get into each other's lives. Be intentional, be real, and be ready for a blessing.

1. What did you learn from this week's set of devotions?

2. What changes need to take place in your life because of this?

3. What steps of faith are you taking to make those changes?

4. Select at least one verse from this week to memorize. Explain why you chose that verse and how it applies to you.

Whereas the truth of God's Word has been opposed, and the execution of His will obstructed in my life: Now, therefore, I, _____, a redeemed child of God, in virtue of the power of the Holy Spirit who in me resides, do hereby formally declare war against impurity and the sinful desires of my flesh which are battling against my soul (1 Pet. 2:11; Jas. 4:1; Gal. 5:17).

In this state of conflict, it is resolved and determined that I will put to death the misdeeds of my body (Rom. 8:13). I therefore do assert and promise before God and the witnesses whose signatures are affixed below that:

- I WILL from this point forward take full responsibility for my thoughts, words, and actions;
- I WILL learn from my mistakes, repent of my sins, and endeavor to be holy in all of my thoughts, words, and actions (Eph. 1:4; 1 Pet. 1:15-16);
- I WILL seek first God's kingdom and righteousness in every aspect of my life (Matt. 6:33);
- I WILL daily (Ac. 17:11) invest my time in the study and meditation of God's Word, turning my ear to God's wisdom and applying my heart to understanding His Truth (Prov. 2:2-3);
- I WILL treasure (Job 23:12) and memorize God's Word, and daily apply its truth and standards to my life (Psa. 119:9, 11, 97, 105), being a doer of the Word and not a hearer only (Jas. 1:25);
- I WILL be a man who always endeavors to walk before God in integrity (1 Ki. 9:4; Psa. 25:21; Prov. 10:9);
- I WILL endeavor to set my mind only on those things that glorify God (Col. 3:2; Phil. 4:8);
- I WILL strive to take captive every thought and make each one fully obedient to Christ (2 Cor. 10:5);
- I WILL daily prepare my mind for battle, I WILL be self-controlled and I WILL set my hope for victory fully on Christ (1 Pet. 1:13);
- I WILL control my own body in a way that is honorable, abstaining from the sinful desires of my flesh (1 Pet. 2:11) and avoiding all forms of sexual immorality (1 Thess. 4:3-4);
- I WILL NOT look lustfully at a woman (Job 31:1; Prov. 6:25; Matt. 5:28);
- I WILL NOT allow even a hint of sexual immorality, or any kind of impurity be in me (Eph. 5:3);
- I WILL NOT allow my TV, computer, or handheld devices, movies, books, magazines, or any other form of entertainment to set before my eyes any ungodly image or standard (Psa. 25:15; 101:2-3; Ezek. 20:7; Num. 33:55; Rom. 16:17; 1 Thess. 5:21-22);
- I WILL always strive to love God with all my heart, with all my soul, with all my mind, and with all my strength (Mark 12:30);
- I WILL fight the good fight, I WILL finish the race, I WILL keep the faith (2 Tim. 4:7).

26261036R00070

Made in the USA
Lexington, KY
21 December 2018